North Idaho's
Lake Country

Text and Photography by George Wuerthner

American & World Geographic Publishing

Above: Lake Pend Oreille from Scotchman Peak.

Title page: Priest Lake State Forest in the Selkirk Mountains.

Front cover: Lake Pend Oreille from Minerva Point.

Back cover (top): Moyie River near Meadow Creek.

Back cover (bottom): Hills Resort, Priest Lake.

Library of Congress Cataloging-in-Publication Data

Wuerthner, George.
    North Idaho's Lake Country / text and photography by George Wuerthner.
        p.   cm.
    Includes index.
    ISBN 1-56037-079-3 (paperback)
    1. Idaho--History, Local. 2. Idaho--Geography. 3. Geology--Idaho. I. Title.
F746.W84 1995   95-14568
979.6--dc20

Text and Photography ©1995 George Wuerthner
© 1995 American & World Geographic Publishing

Write for our catalog:

American & World Geographic Publishing
P.O. Box 5630, Helena, MT 59604

Printed in U.S.A.

Left: Benewah Lake in Heyburn State Park west of St. Maries.

Below: Palouse country, seen here near Worley.

Above: Wild rose along the Kootenai River.

Facing page: Sunset over Priest Lake.

Contents

Right: Beauty Bay, Coeur d'Alene Lake.

Below: Spanning the Moyie River by Moyie Springs.

Facing page: Western redcedar along the St. Joe Wild and Scenic River.

I wrote this book to familiarize people with the human and natural history of North Idaho's Lake Country, as well as some of the attractions and attributes that resident and visitor alike find appealing. It is meant to provide just enough geology to interpret the landscape, just enough history to understand the events that shaped the human endeavors, and just enough geographic material to comprehend how it all fits together.

Preface

Above: The golf course and famous floating green at the Coeur d'Alene Resort.

Left: City Beach Park, Coeur d'Alene, dressed in summer garb.

Facing page: The popular Coeur d'Alene Resort.

Copper Falls in the Purcell Mountains, Kaniksu National Forest.

T wenty thousand years ago, when the giant lobe of the Purcell Trench Glacier ground its way south out of Canada, it created a landscape that humans would find particularly inviting. Upon its retreat back north, a rich legacy of lakes, glacier-scoured peaks, and a fertile, flat outwash plain remained. This land of glacier-spawned lakes, thick evergreen forests and rumpled mountains is North Idaho's Lake Country. All of this landscape diversity is tightly packed into a compact region.

Along its northern border, Lake Country is a mere 45 miles wide. If it were not for the mountains that rise up in your way, you could drive across the state in less than an hour. From the Canadian border to the St. Joe River is about 130 miles. Two states border Lake Country—Washington on the west, and Montana on the east, while British Columbia, Canada, forms the northern border.

Lake Country seems different from almost any other section of the Rocky Mountain West. You almost feel like you're in New England instead of the Rockies. That illusion persists in spite of such non-New England features as grizzly bears and groves of giant Western redcedar.

Part of the sensation has to do with the water. The Rocky Mountain region is relatively arid. Indeed, early travelers referred to the plains and the Rockies beyond as the Great American Desert. And certainly, if you visit southern Idaho, the sagebrush and grass valleys confirm this impression. That notion, however, is quickly forgotten among the fern-lined creeks and timbered slopes of Lake Country's mountains.

Looking at a map, you see that the most dominant landscape features are the big water bodies—Coeur d'Alene Lake, Lake Pend Oreille (pronounced Pon-der-*ray*), and Priest Lake. Lake Pend Oreille qualifies as immense—nearly 65 miles long at its extreme length, and 15 miles wide at its greatest girth. There are few natural lakes in the West that rival it in size: Flathead in Montana, Tahoe in California-Nevada, and Salt Lake in Utah.

1 An Overview

Western redcedar along Myrtle Creek.

The Western redcedar swarms Lake Country landscape, here along the Moyie River near Meadow Creek.

Those lakes are more or less by themselves. What makes the area distinctive is that its bodies of water are set in a matrix of dozens of smaller lakes dotting the valleys, including Twin Lakes, Spirit Lake, Hauser Lake, Fernan Lake, Cocolalla Lake, Upper Priest Lake, Rose Lake and Hayden Lake. And this litany doesn't include the dozens of alpine lakes nestled among the mountains.

Though lakes are the region's most distinguishing features, rivers and streams carve the landscape. There is the remote Moyie River, once lined by towns that are now gone. The deep and serene Kootenai winds through fertile farmland. The Coeur

d'Alene flows through the most mineral-rich valley in America. And at the south end is the shadowy St. Joe, a designated Wild and Scenic river, whose headwaters rise in the wildest country in North Idaho. There are other rivers as well—the Pack, Priest, Pend Oreille and Clark Fork. All of them contribute to a sense of otherness—a section of the well-watered East set among western woods.

Yet this isn't just like northern Minnesota or Maine—they have lots of lakes and rivers too. What's special about Lake Country is that these waters are positioned among hills and mountains. The most famous mountains are the granite-ribbed Selkirks. They dominate the northwest corner of the region. Part of a much larger range that makes up the Columbia Ranges in British Columbia, the Selkirks of Idaho are about 100 miles long. They were heavily glaciated during the last Ice Age and have an abundance of cirque lakes and U-shaped valleys.

This wheat field at sunset below the Selkirk Mountains near Bonners Ferry attests to the area's rich land.

To the east of the Selkirks, and northeast of Bonners Ferry, and drained by the Moyie River, are the Purcell Mountains. The Purcells are the southern fringe of yet another British Columbian range that is higher and more dramatic in Canada. At the southern end in Idaho, the highest point in the Purcells is about a thousand feet lower than the Selkirks. Unlike the granitic Selkirks, the Purcells are composed primarily of metamorphic Belt Rocks.

Between the Kootenai River and the Clark Fork River along the border of Montana are the Cabinet Mountains. The highest summit, Scotchman Peak, barely tops 7,000 feet. Nevertheless, the peak rises nearly 5,000 feet above the valley. The views from its craggy summit present a spectacular vista of Montana as well as Lake Pend Oreille spread out below.

South of the Clark Fork River and north of Interstate 90 lie the Coeur d'Alene Mountains, a broad plateau that has been dissected by rivers. The highest point, Grizzly Mountain, attains a height of 5,950 feet. Interstate 90 follows the Coeur d'Alene River Valley, which also marks the Osborn Fault. The fault has moved the sedimentary and metamorphic rocks of this range more than 16 miles. In the process, numerous cracks developed that filled with liquid mineral-laden rock, which later formed the basis of northern Idaho's silver and gold mining industry. Early miners scratched at the earth to take away the mineral wealth; then large companies bored into the mountains and left behind a legacy of heavy metal pollution that was never figured in the cost of mining operations. Today the Coeur d'Alene valley is one of the biggest environmental cleanup sites in the United States.

Lying between the Coeur d'Alene River and the St. Joe River are the St. Joe Mountains. The highest summit, Latour Peak, is 6,308 feet. Although the crest barely exceeds 6,000 feet, the regrowth from the massive 1910 forest fires gives the range an alpine character. The upper St. Joe drainage is part of the north and central Idaho "elk factory." The shrubs that invaded the burned slopes provides the browse that has sustained impressive elk herds for decades. This is one of the least visited and wildest parts of North Idaho.

Most of these mountain ranges are under U.S. Forest Service management. The three forests—the Kaniksu, Coeur d'Alene and St. Joe—were combined under one management and renamed the Panhandle National Forest. The Bureau of Land Management (BLM) also manages some land, particularly along

TIM CHRISTIE

Above: Lake Coeur d'Alene, from Canfield Mountain.

Facing page (top): Kootenai National Wildlife Refuge.

Bottom: Palouse Prairie sunrise.

Mule deer in cedar forest along Priest Lake.

the shores of Lake Coeur d'Alene. The Coeur d'Alene tribe is a major landowner, and the state of Idaho too has some large holdings, including Priest Lake State Forest, which takes much of the western slope of the Selkirk Mountains from the shore of Priest Lake to the mountain crest.

Some of Lake Country's counties are largely in federal or state ownership. For example, 73 percent of Boundary County is under state or federal management. Since federal lands are not taxed, the federal government helps local governments meet their financial commitments through PILT (Payment in Lieu of Taxes) payments. In most cases, PILT payments are higher than the taxes paid on similar private holdings.

Since these lands are owned by all citizens, there are almost as many opinions over how to manage them as there are people. Questions about how much logging is too much, which areas should remain roadless and be protected as designated wilderness, and how to save endangered species are all discussed with a fervor usually reserved for debates between fans of rival basketball teams.

There is good reason for this contention. Lake Country has some of the most magnificent and most productive forests in the Rockies. At lower elevations grow ponderosa pine and Douglas-fir. On wetter sites, you might find paper birch, a species more common in New England and the upper Midwest. Along rivers grow beautiful stands of black cottonwood, amidst a host of understory shrubs. At slightly higher elevations are forests of western larch. The larch flares golden in the autumn, bringing much color to the otherwise dark evergreen forests. In moist areas with deep soils grow huge Western redcedar. Some groves have especially large specimens that rival small redwoods in size. Mixed with the cedar are Western hemlock and grand-fir forests—both species tolerant of shade. Among the subalpine reaches are lodgepole pine and subalpine-fir forests. Engelmann spruce is another common mid-elevation species. The highest snowy ridgelines, such as Silver Peak by Kellogg, have stands of mountain hemlock. Also found on rocky ridgelines are whitebark pine, whose cones are especially sought after by bears as food.

Perhaps the most distinctive tree in all of Lake Country is the Western white pine. This was the king of the timber trees. Though found throughout the Cascades and the Sierra Nevada, the tree reached its most graceful and largest size here. When the timber industry moved to Idaho, it came for the white pine. Western white pine grows tall and straight, with a fine-grain wood. A fire-adapted species, it quickly reinvades a site after fire. Unfortunately, not only were most of the larger stands of white pine cut out, but also white pine blister rust, a disease introduced from Europe, has devastated the remaining pine forests. Fortunately, some trees are resistant to the disease, and over time, Western white pine might regain a foothold.

Since logging began in the region, nearly all the private timber company holdings have been cut at least once, and most of the federal lands have also been logged. With the increase in timber harvest, there has been a huge increase in forest roading. On just the Panhandle National Forest alone, there are more than 10,000 miles of logging roads, making it difficult to get more than a few miles from a road almost anywhere in the entire region.

Above: Western redcedar bole, along Snow Creek.

Top: Near Murray in the Coeur d'Alene Mountains. A gold rush to Murray died out by 1885, but miners fanned out into the countryside.

Increasingly, people see forests as more than a woodpile. These timbered slopes are also home to dozens of species. Unlike much of the rest of the country, Lake Country is fortunate to have most of the species that were here when the first white explorers appeared, although some exist at perilously low numbers. While not everywhere abundant, mountain goat, moose, elk, whitetail deer, mule deer, marten, wolverine, lynx, mountain lion, grizzly bear, black bear, beaver, marmot, pika, badger, and a host of other species are still seen.

Elk in particular have sustained a spectacular recovery from turn-of-the-20th-century lows. Market hunting for the mining camps, plus year-round unregulated subsistence hunting had taken its toll on big-game numbers. In the early 1900s it was difficult to find elk anywhere. For example, in one of the first game counts, only one elk was reported in Lake Country. The elk season was completely closed in 1911 and did not reopen again until 1945. And it was not until 1955 that elk hunting was permitted throughout North Idaho.

The change in elk numbers was the result of several factors: protection from hunters hastened recovery; shrub regrowth after the major forest fires in 1910 and 1919 provided the brushy habi-

St. Joe River below Conrad Crossing, Panhandle National Forest.

tat that elk favor; and, beginning in 1919, the Shoshone Sportmen's Association began to plant elk in northern Idaho. Between 1919 and 1939, 256 elk were released.

Other species have not fared as well. Today, Lake Country is one of the last outposts for a host of species found in few other parts of the country. The woodland caribou, once ranging in Idaho as far south as Grangeville, is now restricted to a small part of the Selkirk Mountains. Its population is declining. Similarly, the grizzly bear is down to a couple of dozen, primarily in the Selkirks, with a few in the Purcell Mountains along the Montana border.

Gray wolves occasionally wander into Lake Country. Their presence will likely increase as recovery efforts in Montana proceed. There is also concern for the welfare of the lynx, wolverine, and fisher. All of these species are predators that exist in very low numbers and range widely to survive.

And the Kootenai River white sturgeon, recently listed as endangered, is suffering because of dam construction on the Kootenai River in Montana that has eliminated the deep spring flows the species requires for successful regeneration. Another native fish, the bull trout, is likewise in trouble. Its numbers have declined dramatically. Sedimentation from logging roads destroys spawning habitat. In addition, degraded habitat favors the nonnative brook trout, which then out-competes the bull trout.

Not all species, however, are suffering declines. Bald eagles and osprey are on the upswing—both fish eaters that were near extinction due to pesticide poisoning.

The recovery of endangered or threatened species is not without controversy. Caribou and grizzly are often shot, even with full protection under the Endangered Species Act. In addition, the caribou requires old-growth forest for survival—an increasingly rare commodity in a region with heavy timber production. Protection of bull trout habitat might require curbs on logging. Of course, while there are costs, there are benefits that go beyond saving any particular animal from extinction. Protecting the habitat for these species helps to maintain functioning ecosystems as well—something that benefits all humans.

And it is quality of life, more than anything, that gives distinction to Lake Country. All this water, wildlife, forests, and mountains make an intimacy that contrasts with southern Idaho's spacious sagebrush deserts. I think of it as Idaho's New England. Modest farms tucked back in the hills help to maintain a rural flavor and the small towns like Priest River, Spirit Lake, St. Maries, Bonners Ferry and Clark Fork give this region a singular character. Lake Country is a complex mix of old mining ruins and new ski resorts. Loggers and downhill skiers. Farms and high-tech industry. Today all of these mix in the Lake Country landscape; however, it was not always such a mixture.

For years Lake Country was the domain of the logger, for good reason. What you feel here, more than anything else, is the forest. Tall stands of Western redcedar, Douglas-fir, Western larch, and Western white pine don't just grow on the mountains, rather they swarm over the landscape. Although the region was first exploited for furs and gold, timber came to dominate the regional economy for decades.

Now logging is giving way to tourism as the region's and the state's largest industry. According to one study, tourism generated $1.3 billion for Idaho's economy in 1994. The largest percentage of visitors come from nearby Washington, but Californians tallied a close second.

It's easy to understand why. Between the snowy slopes at Schweitzer Basin, Lookout Pass and Silver Peak that lure ski buffs in winter and the water-focused summer of fishing, swimming and boating, there is never a shortage of reasons to be outdoors. People come to view bald eagles near Coeur d'Alene and to mountain-bike the miles of logging roads in the Selkirks. Some communities such as Coeur d'Alene and Sandpoint are dominated by the tourist industry, while others such as Kellogg and Bonners Ferry seem poised to make that leap.

Retirees and escapees from the urban jungle are also moving into the region in ever increasing numbers. In 1994 more out-of-state residents moved to Coeur d'Alene and the surrounding Kootenai County than to any other county in the state except Ada County, where Boise is located. Of the 33,000 people who exchanged their out-of-state drivers' licenses for Idaho licenses, 14 percent now live in Kootenai County, and another 5 percent live in Bonner County, where Sandpoint is located. Former Californians lead the pack, but residents of Oregon and Washington also were part of this immigration.

Statistics tell the story. Kootenai County's 1960 population was 29,556. By 1990 it had jumped to 69,795. This growth has

Cottonwood in autumn at Carlin Bay, Coeur d'Alene Lake.

Above: Lake Pend Oreille from the summit of Scotchman Peak.

Top: Looking across the Purcell Trench to the Selkirk Mountains.

created more jobs—primarily in the service sector. The economy becomes an "I'll scratch your back if you'll scratch mine" affair. The school teacher needs a banker, plumber and doctor. They all send their kids to a school. All buy groceries at the supermarket. And so it goes.

One important new economic force is the group of people choosing Lake Country for retirement. Retirement and other transfer payments are not tracked by county "employment" figures. In many parts of the West such funds account for as much as 50 percent of the economic activity, but the economic effect of this massive transfer of income is often underestimated or ignored. Yet, this influx of people adds support to new businesses and services.

Again using Kootenai County as an example, of a total non-agricultural employment in 1990 of 25,000 jobs, 6,772 were in the wholesale and retail trade, another 5,543 were in services, and if you add in finance, insurance, real estate, transportation and communications there are another 2,300 jobs. By contrast, the lumber and wood products industry employed only 1,853 Kootenai County residents in 1990, and the number has dropped since that time. And though you get the impression from grumbling you hear in the small-town cafes that most people in Lake Country don't like "big government," federal, state, county and local bureaucracies employ 5,200 county residents. Without government jobs a major source of economic stability would be lost.

Some suggest that Kootenai County, which includes the rapidly growing communities of Post Falls and Coeur d'Alene, are not truly representative of the "real" North Idaho. But even Boundary County, which includes Bonners Ferry, has seen similar shifts in population and economics, though of a smaller magnitude. For example, in the past ten years, Boundary County has gained a thousand new residents. That may not seem like much compared to Kootenai County, which got more than 4,000 new residents in one year. However, when you consider that Boundary County has only a little more than 9,000 residents, an increase of 1,000 people is a significant jump.

Boundary County is even more dependent upon government employment for economic stability. In 1990, more than 700 people (28 percent) out of a total workforce of 2,500 were employed in government. The wood products industry is proportionately more important here, but is still overshadowed by the service industry.

Not everyone is happy with the state of affairs. While the availability of jobs increases, there are other costs to being the playground and retirement home for the rest of the country or state. Congestion and crime rise. Some of the very features that attract people may be degraded. For example, the Environmental Protection Agency (EPA) has warned Sandpoint residents that breathing their "pure" mountain air may now be a health risk—mostly as a result of dust and woodstove smoke—a common problem in many northern Idaho mountain communities. Population growth can cause a community to lose the small-town intimacy of knowing neighbors and the folks met on the street. Housing prices often escalate, sometimes beyond the reach of longtime residents. Still, the alternative is often worse. Many former Lake Country communities, such as Klockman and Crossport, are nothing more than moldering logs in the forest. Typically, a place with low housing costs is also a place with high unemployment, few job opportunities, and an out-migration of young people.

While some people complain about the crowds at Coeur d'Alene and Sandpoint, Lake Country isn't crowded. Consider that Vermont, a state approximately the same size as North Idaho's Lake Country, has more than 600,000 people. Yet Vermont is considered one of the most rural states in the nation. What disturbs some about Lake Country's current boom is the resulting sprawl and growing congestion. In other parts of the country planning and zoning have maintained the rural character that continues to draw people, while still permitting guided development.

Lake Country residents appear vigorously opposed to infringement upon their right to do as they wish with their property. At the same time, some residents also bemoan the loss of the rural character they love about their corner of the state.

2
The
Formation

One of the defining geological structures in all of Idaho lies near Bonners Ferry. The best place to see it is from Highway 95 a couple of miles south of town. The long, narrow valley, bounded by the Selkirks on one side and the Purcells on the other, is the giant trough of the Purcell Trench.

The Purcell Trench is a structural fault or giant crack in the earth's crust that runs from northern Idaho up into British Columbia for hundreds of miles. How the trench came to be is explained, in part, by the origins of the Selkirks. The granites that make up the Selkirks were formed deep in the earth. So how did they get to be exposed on the earth's surface? Not only exposed, but elevated? Let it suffice for now to say that they were uplifted, and that the overlying rocks that once buried them were tilted off and actually slid eastward across the valley. They now make up the rocks of the Purcell and Cabinet mountains. The Purcell Trench marks the division between these two rock types.

To imagine that entire mountain ranges can slide across the landscape is difficult enough, but the rocks making up the Purcells and Cabinets have their own outrageous histories as well. These rocks are members of the Belt Super Group, or Belt Rocks for short. They formed more than a billion years ago. That's a span of time difficult to process in our brains, but it's well before dinosaurs—indeed well before most forms of life had evolved at all.

Interestingly, the Belt formation rocks appear to end abruptly at what is now the Idaho border. Rocks of similar age, structure and other characteristics are found in Asia. Some geologists speculate that the western part of North America broke off and drifted toward what is now Asia and were welded onto that land mass. The rocks that now make up eastern Washington were rafted into position along the old edge of the North America plate and plastered onto the continent later.

The Belt Rocks are named for the Belt Mountains of central Montana, where they were first discovered. They are not that common in central Montana; they do, however, make up the bulk of the rocks found in Idaho and western Montana. Most

Above: Field of mustard in the Purcell Trench below the Purcell Mountains.

Facing page: Granite boulders line Pack River in the Selkirk Mountains.

people are familiar with Belt Rocks if they have ever viewed the colorful red rocks found in Glacier National Park in Montana. Indeed, if you want to identify the bedrock anywhere in Lake Country outside of the Selkirks, you would be pretty safe in saying it was some kind of Belt stone.

The Belt Rocks are composed of sediments—mud and sands—that likely collected in sea basins. These deposits are now over 40,000 feet thick. Over time these sediments were metamorphosed into rock—shales, mudstones and sandstones. Then they were metamorphosed further, into argillites, quartzites, and siltites.

The named formations of the Belt Rocks, from oldest to youngest, are the Prichard, Burke, Revett, St. Regis, Wallace, Striped Peak, and Libby formations. The names correspond to the place names of where outcrops were first studied. The Burke formation was first studied near Burke, Idaho, the Libby formation near Libby, Montana, and so forth.

Geologists speculate that these rocks formed under conditions vastly different from those of today. The earth's atmosphere had little oxygen—which we breathe—and mostly carbon dioxide, which we exhale. Carbon dioxide effectively traps heat—the global warming phenomenon. High air temperature results in greater humidity. The earth at this time was warm and humid. Little life, except blue-green algae, existed. Over time, however, these blue-green algae converted carbon dioxide into oxygen. About 570 million years ago, at the end of the Precambrian Era ("precambrian" means before life) enough oxygen existed to permit an explosion of oxygen-breathing life. Thus, the Belt Rocks mark the end of the simple-cell life forms that dominated the earth, and the transitional point where higher life as we know it began to evolve rapidly on earth.

Intruded into these Belt Rocks are sills. Sills are horizontal (like window sills; hence the name) rock layers that form when any kind of molten magma is squeezed into existing rock fractures and later hardens into place. Most of the sills in northern Idaho are several hundred feet thick.

The Selkirk Mountains are the exposed part of the Kaniksu Batholith. Batholiths, which form deep in the earth, are composed of magma emplaced beneath overlying younger rocks. The magma that created the Kaniksu Batholith was intruded some 70 to 80 million years ago, towards the end of the reign of dinosaurs. At the same time, the granitic batholiths that are now exposed in the Bitterroot Mountains and Salmon River Mountains of central Idaho were also being formed.

Just south of Newport and north of Post Falls lies the Spokane Dome, which includes Mount Spokane in Washington. The Spokane Dome is a smaller outcrop of granitic rock formed in the same manner as the Kaniksu Batholith. Its eastern flank is marked by the Purcell Trench fault. This smaller mass of granitic rock is approximately the same age as the granite in the Kaniksu Batholith, and most geologists believe they are related.

The upward pressure exerted by the rising magma caused some of the overlying rock strata to break loose and slide eastward—the Belt Rocks that now make up the Purcell and Cabinet mountains. There are some small granitic masses in both of these mountain ranges that appear to be pieces of the Kaniksu Batholith that slid eastward with the Belt Rocks.

South of Sandpoint lie the Coeur d'Alene Mountains. The mountains are not very high, nor as dramatic as those farther north in Idaho, but they held some of the richest mineral deposits in the West. Apparently the Belt Rocks making up the Coeur d'Alene Mountains developed a lot of fractures. Into these fractures, superheated water with mineral concentrate was intruded. These cooled to create mineral veins loaded with silver, gold and other valuable metals that made the Coeur d'Alene mines world-famous. Eighty percent of the ore mined in Idaho came from these mines. Gold was discovered as a placer deposit here in 1881, but it was silver that brought fame. More than a billion ounces of silver have come from the mines. In addition to silver, gold, lead, zinc, and copper were also produced within the Coeur d'Alene mining district.

Between Lookout Pass and Coeur d'Alene, I-90 follows the Coeur d'Alene River. Both the river and the highway are remarkably straight considering that they wind through a major mountain uplift. Their relatively direct path is due to the Osborn Fault, a major structural break in the earth's crust. The grinding of rock along the fault broke it up, making it easier for the river to erode it. The valley of the Clark Fork River farther north follows yet another structural fault—the Hope Fault. In general, all of the region's rivers, as well as most of the towns and highways, are along major structural faults because that is where erosional forces had the best opportunities for removing fractured rock.

Sunset on Priest Lake from near Camels Prairie Lookout.

The faults dictated the underlying geological setting, but the icing on the cake, so to speak, was glaciation. During the past two million years (humans have been on earth during this entire period) a number of Ice Ages have come and gone. Only the remains of the two most recent are readily evident—one from about 100,000 years ago, and the more contemporary glaciation that ended only 10,000 years ago.

During the height of the glacial period, ice sheets formed over the mountains in British Columbia and giant valley glaciers slowly oozed their way south in northern Idaho, completely filling the Purcell Trench. Eventually this mass of ice overrode all but the highest summits. The ice was at least 4,000 feet thick.

The terminal end of the glacier lay just north of Coeur d'Alene. In addition to this thick lobe of continental ice, cirque glaciers formed in many of the higher lake basins, particularly in the Selkirk and Cabinet mountains.

All of the higher peaks in the Selkirk, Purcell, Cabinet, Coeur d'Alene and St. Joe mountains experienced some level of glaciation. As glaciers move slowly down the mountain, they pluck at the rock beneath. As a result, they gradually carve out bowl-like basins called cirques. Sometimes water collects in these bowls to form cirque lakes. The scalloped, smoothed Selkirk crest has dozens of cirque lakes and basins.

If a cirque glacier grows large enough, it might spill out of its basin and flow down the adjacent valley. A glaciated valley typically has steep sides and a nearly flat bottom, which gives a characteristic U-shape. Some of the best examples of glaciated U-shaped valleys can be seen in the Selkirks. The headwaters of Myrtle Creek, Long Canyon, and Pack River are good examples of glacier-scoured valleys.

Debris imbedded in the bottom of the moving glacier rasps at the bedrock as it moves, smoothing the rock like a giant grinder. Some of the higher peaks in the Selkirks display a tremendous amount of this glacial grinding and polishing.

As glaciers move downslope, they collect broken rock, dirt, and other materials scraped from the side of mountains or ground under the weight of moving ice. This rock, which is called moraine, is pushed along the glacier's margins. Basically, moraines are just piles of dirt transported and shaped by glaciers. Moraines are abundant throughout Lake Country, but are sometimes difficult to see due to the vegetation that covers so much of the landscape. Sometimes the moraine dams the flow of a river, creating a lake. A moraine dam is partially responsible for Priest Lake.

Once the glaciers retreated, a huge amount of glacial debris and outwash was redistributed across what is now the Rathdrum Prairie and the valley of the Purcell Trench. The relatively flat surface of these valleys reflects this glacial past.

The region's lakes also owe their existence to glaciers. Priest Lake lies in a glacier-scoured basin as does Lake Pend Oreille. Pend Oreille's great depth—over 1,000 feet deep—is unusual. Geologists speculate that a huge lobe of ice remained in the basin after the main body had retreated. The ice block kept the lake basin from filling up with sediments. Although the Purcell Trench is lower in elevation than Pend Oreille, recessional moraines kept the lake from emptying northward into the Kootenai River.

Although glaciers carved most of the lakes in northern Idaho, the Coeur d'Alene Lake basin was never glaciated. Nevertheless, the lake owes its existence to the Ice Age glaciers. Prior to the last two major glacial periods, the St. Joe River flowed north through today's Coeur d'Alene to Rathdrum Prairie. Terminal moraine and other debris left by the retreating glacier just north of the town of Coeur d'Alene blocked the northward flow of the St. Joe, creating the lake.

During the glacial maximum there were two major ice sheets covering North America—the Laurentian, which covered most of eastern Canada and the northeast United States, and the Cordilleran, which covered the mountains of British Columbia. The giant glacial lobe of the Cordilleran ice sheet that filled the Purcell Trench waxed and waned. It occasionally blocked the flow of the Clark Fork River. Each time, the ice dam backed up water to form Glacial Lake Missoula. The lake was named for the city of Missoula, in Montana, where ancient lake shores are still visible on the surrounding hillsides. At times, Glacial Lake Missoula was more than 2,000 feet deep. However, ice will float. The rising lake waters eventually floated the ice dam, sending a wall of water 2,000 feet deep surging towards the Pacific. This occurred more than 40 times. Each time the ice dam burst, the lake emptied in a matter of days, unleashing the greatest floods ever known on earth.

The floods were so great and so rapid that icebergs from northern Idaho were rafted across eastern Washington and down the Columbia River to surge up Oregon's Willamette Valley. Some of these flood-propelled icebergs traveled upstream as far as 80 miles from today's Portland. There are granite boulders in the Willamette Valley transported from northern Idaho by these periodic floods. The main path of the floods was through the Rathdrum Prairie and Spokane Valley. Flood waters flowed down the Pend Oreille River valley as well.

Most of the major landscape features were in place after the last glaciers retreated. Since that time, rivers have cut channels into the sediments that once covered the valleys, creating terraces and benches. These terraces are readily seen along the Kootenai River north of Bonners Ferry. The rich soils are excellent for farming.

Geologists believe we are currently in an interglacial warming period, and it is only a matter of time before the ice returns. Recent research shows that the return of an ice age can be remarkably rapid—a matter of a few hundred years. Whether we are heading toward a new Ice Age or if global warming will send us off on another path, no one knows.

3
Historical
Glimpses

The first people to venture into northern Idaho were referred to as Paleo-Indians. Big-game hunters seeking woolly mammoth and giant bison, they left behind evidence of their presence in the form of spear-points and bones, but not much else. They arrived sometime after the last ice sheets were retreating northward. Humans were always on the move, and in all likelihood, the indigenous people living in Idaho at the time of white exploration were not direct descendants of these earlier inhabitants. People shifted their territories in response to changing climate, food availability, and pressures from other people. Nevertheless, in the most recent past, northern Idaho was largely populated by recent immigrants.

Cottonwood along Coeur d'Alene Lake.

For example, the Kutenai Indians are linguistically unrelated to any other Idaho tribes. They were originally plains dwellers from the east who were pushed into northern Idaho by the powerful Blackfeet. The Pend d'Oreille (also called Kalispells) and Coeur d'Alene tribes, however, were immigrants from the west, moving up the Columbia River and its tributaries. Both of these tribes relied upon roots like camas lily for food, as well as on fishing and hunting. In 1800 there were an estimated 6,000 to 10,000 Indians living in Idaho. In all of northern Idaho there were not many more than a thousand people—some 700 Coeur d'Alene, 300 Pend d'Oreille, and 200 or so Kutenai.

Into this arrangement came the first whites. Between 1804 and 1806, the Lewis and Clark expedition traipsed from St. Louis, Missouri, to the mouth of the Columbia and back again, crossing Idaho twice in the process. They were the first Europeans to see Idaho. Indeed, Idaho was the last of the future states Euro-Americans reached. Lewis and Clark took careful notes on

all aspects of the landscape, but their frequent comments on the abundance of beaver along western streams had the most immediate impact upon the land. The news of the beaver drew hundreds of fur trappers into the Rocky Mountain region.

The next white known to visit Idaho was Canadian, the intrepid David Thompson of the North West Company based in Montreal. Thompson ranged far and wide across southern Canada, western Montana and into northern Idaho, trading with the Indians and scouting out trading possibilities. In 1808, Thompson traded with Indians near Bonners Ferry. The following year, he returned to northern Idaho and set up a trading post named Kullyspell House on the shores of Lake Pend Oreille. A few years later, Thompson also built Spokane House near present-

Wetlands at Kootenai National Wildlife Refuge by Bonners Ferry.

day Spokane. This post was more successful, soon superseding Kullyspell House, which was abandoned. A highway sign near Hope marks the general location of Kullyspell House today.

The Hudson's Bay Company eventually took over the Canadian fur operations, which included all of Idaho and the rest of the Pacific Northwest. The fur trade opened up the major routes of travel through the landscape, putting names on the map, and providing the outside world its first descriptions of Idaho.

Although there were occasional skirmishes between trappers and Indians, overall the fur trade didn't pose a direct threat to Indians' way of life. Trappers were few, and many took Native American spouses and assumed a lifestyle similar to that of the indigenous people. The implements Indian people obtained in trade, such as metal knives, blankets, sewing needles, and pots, made life easier, but the increasing trade with whites had a less desirable side to it. Most Native Americans had little resistance to diseases such as smallpox and even measles. Entire villages were depopulated when these European diseases reached a region. Even before Lewis and Clark had ventured into Idaho and Oregon, native people had suffered huge die-offs from diseases they caught from passing European trade expeditions plying the coast of North America in the late 1700s. Then, through intertribal trade, warfare, and contacts, the diseases were spread from tribe to tribe across the Pacific Northwest with deadly consequences. Although the Indian Wars are glorified in white history books, it was disease that subdued and destroyed Indian culture and often led to the destabilization of tribal territories.

The mixing of fur trappers with Indians stimulated the interests of some Native Americans for European religion. In 1831, a delegation of Nez Perce Indians and one Flathead Indian traveled to St. Louis to request a mission for their people. Presbyterian missionaries were sent westward in response. Between 1834 and 1838, a number of missions were established in the Northwest, including a Presbyterian mission on the Clearwater River near present-day Lewiston. The Catholic mission established among the Coeur d'Alene people near Saint Maries in 1842 was the earliest in Lake Country. Due to flooding at the first site, the mission was moved in 1846 to Cataldo. By 1844 another mission to serve the Kalispell, or Pend d'Oreille, Indians was also operating on the Pend Oreille River near the Idaho-Washington border.

One of the more famous Jesuit missionaries, Father Anthony Ravalli, who operated St. Mary's Mission in the Bitterroot Valley of Montana, moved to the mission at Cataldo in 1850. The missionaries persuaded the Indians to become farmers and homesteaders and to adopt European religion. In effect, they may have eroded the Indian culture more than the cavalry, the hordes of miners, and others who followed, though with less malice.

The opening of the missionary era signaled the end of another era. Due to heavy trapping, beaver had dwindled to near extinction. This, along with a change in fashion, caused a collapse in the fur market by the early 1840s. Just as this was occurring, however, the opening of the Oregon Trail in 1842 created a new impetus for western expansion.

Idaho was at the time part of Oregon Territory, which was still officially under British rule. In 1848, the U.S. government negotiated a treaty with Britain establishing the 49th parallel (the present border of Canada and the U.S.) as the northern limits of U.S. territory in the Pacific Northwest. Oregon Territory included all of what are now the states of Washington, Oregon, Idaho and part of western Montana, and even northwest Wyoming. In 1853, Oregon Territory was sliced off of Washington Territory along the Columbia River. Northern Idaho then became part of Washington Territory, while southern Idaho was still part of Oregon. In 1859, Oregon became a state and assumed its present boundaries. All of Idaho was then reunited as part of Washington Territory. In 1863, Washington Territory assumed the present state boundaries and Idaho then extended east across today's Montana. Finally, in 1868, Idaho's boundaries assumed their present shape when the Wyoming border was pushed west.

All of this territorial adjustment was the result of western expansion. Beginning in the 1840s and throughout the 1850s, and even during the Civil War years of the 1860s, settlers, miners, and others moved west in record numbers. Settlers bound for Oregon traveled across southern Idaho, stopping at old Hudson's Bay posts such as Fort Boise and Fort Hall. The trickle of settlers became a flood after gold was discovered in California in 1848. With the first inkling that minerals might be found in the West, other prospectors began to fan out across the landscape seeking new gold fields. In a few years, they had reached Oregon, and by the 1860s were pushing into Idaho.

Pack River Delta Wildlife Area on Lake Pend Oreille.

In 1860, E.D. Pierce discovered gold on the Clearwater River. This region was part of the Nez Perce Indian Reservation. By law, miners were not permitted to enter. Pierce, using his trading enterprise as a cover, ventured onto the reservation. He found enough gold on his survey expedition to warrant a modest rush. By 1861, several thousand miners were trespassing on the reservation looking for more of the yellow metal. Finding that they could not halt the miners, the Nez Perce signed another treaty that permitted miners access to lands north of the Clearwater River, but forbade their entry farther south. This treaty was also eventually ignored when gold was found near Elk City on the South Fork of the Clearwater. Within a few years, whites outnumbered Nez Perce on the reservation.

A rush into the Kootenai mining district in British Columbia brought miners through northern Idaho on what became known as the Wildhorse Trail. The trail followed the Pend

Above: The Cataldo mission or Mission of the Sacred Heart, Old Mission State Park.

Left: Kellogg, a Lake Country delight. Part of its economic revival involved the construction of the world's longest gondola, to the top of Silver Mountain ski area.

Oreille River from Washington around Lake Pend Oreille, and up to Bonners Ferry, where it crossed the Kootenai River, then continued up into Canada. Other mining rushes to central and southern Idaho—including to the Boise Basin, Silver City, the Yankee Fork, and Caribou Mountains—kept Idaho a major mining region for the next twenty years. Ironically, it wasn't until the 1880s that miners stopped long enough in their frantic rush to get to the next bonanza to realize that northern Idaho offered substantial mineral opportunities as well. Ultimately, these mineral deposits would prove more profitable and longer lasting than other discoveries before or since.

In 1882 placer gold was discovered in the Coeur d'Alene Mountains. Other discoveries led to the Coeur d'Alene gold rush of 1884. In that year placer gold mining along the North Fork of the Coeur d'Alene River produced $260,000 in gold. This increased to $375,000 the following year. In the same two years, silver-lead deposits were discovered along the South Fork of the Coeur d'Alene River at Burke, Mullan, Polaris, Kellogg and Osborn. These mines soon became the largest producers of silver-lead in the nation. The Bunker Hill Mine, near Kellogg, produced more silver than the entire Comstock Lode in Nevada! The Bunker Hill was only one of many mines in the region. The entire region became known as the "Silver Valley."

The Coeur d'Alene mines boomed once the Northern Pacific Railroad reached them in 1889, making it possible to get heavy mining equipment to the region inexpensively.

The move to lode mining changed the nature of the industry. While placer deposits found in streams could be worked by lone individuals or small groups of prospectors working collectively on a claim, the larger lode mines were labor intensive. Lode mines required tunneling underground and following veins of mineralization for thousands of feet. The ore then had to be crushed and smelted. All of this required capital, heavy and expensive equipment, and a lot of cheap labor. Labor in the form of immigrants, as well as American-born workers, was abundant in western mining communities. Companies demanded long hours for poor wages. In addition, the work was dangerous. Not surprisingly, mining camps soon became hotbeds for labor unrest. Some of the strongest unions in the nation were formed in Idaho.

During the same period, there were ongoing separation struggles in Idaho Territory. Among the factors involved were northern Idaho's remoteness from the territorial capital, Boise, and economic interests different from those of the south. The rugged Salmon River Mountains more or less made north-south travel through the state impossible. Northern Idahoans had easier travel going east and west than heading south to Boise.

As a consequence, many of northern Idaho's residents wanted either to form their own territory or to rejoin Washington Territory. Another faction wanted to join with western Montana, which also had substantial mining operations at Butte, Anaconda and elsewhere. This group wanted to form a new state. In 1886 a bill to annex North Idaho to Washington Territory was actually submitted to Congress. Although one version or another passed one branch of Congress or the other, no version managed to gain approval of both the House and the Senate. The bid to join North Idaho with Washington languished in Congress.

Help from Nevada was in the works. In 1886, Nevada's mining districts were in decline. People were leaving the state. William Stewart, a former U.S. Senator from Nevada, conceived the idea of Nevada annexing southern Idaho Territory. However, most southern Idaho residents were opposed to the idea. So Stewart tried a different approach. He shepherded a bill through Congress making North Idaho part of Washington. Stewart believed that once North Idaho was split off, southern Idaho would have no choice but to join Nevada. Stewart managed to get the bill through Congress, only to have President Grover Cleveland veto it.

Ultimately, the desire to be part of the United States kept Idaho together. Neither the northern nor the southern part of the state had enough people to qualify as a new state. In order to gain entry into the United States as a state, north and south Idaho had to remain together. Reluctantly, the citizens from both parts of the state worked for admission to the union. July 3, 1890, Idaho became part of the United States, with southern and northern Idaho united.

Around 1900, the emphasis in the region began to shift from minerals to timber. North Idaho's forests began to move into national prominence. The coming of the railroads provided an outlet to markets in the Midwest and East, giving Idaho's abundant forests new commercial value. In addition, in the style of the day, most of the commercial timber in the Great Lakes states had already been cut. The timber industry was looking for new forests. North Idaho was ripe for picking.

Beginning in 1900, Minnesota timberman Frederick Weyerhaeuser, along with other timber barons from the Great Lakes, started buying up North Idaho timberlands. The timber industry's indulgence in the Great Lakes convinced Congress to establish a system of federal forest reserves in the 1890s. When Theodore Roosevelt became president, he greatly enlarged the reserves, organized the U.S. Forest Service, and created the first national forests, many of which were in Idaho. In 1906 much of Idaho's remaining forest land was added to the national forest system by President Roosevelt—much to the displeasure of Idahoans. Idaho's Senator Weldon Heyburn introduced legislation forbidding the president to declare any more national forests. Roosevelt signed the bill, but not before he had set aside another 16 million acres as national forest. Heyburn got even

Above: Ponderosa pine thrive here, along Lake Pend Oreille near Trestle Creek.

Right: Along White Creek north of Wallace.

by denying funding for the first year of the newly established Forest Service.

The timber barons from the Great Lakes who invested heavily in timberlands in Idaho discovered that having trees was one thing, getting them to market economically was another. The steep terrain in northern Idaho made logging expensive. In those days, nearly all logs were transported out of the woods on rail lines. It was expensive to build rails up the steep, narrow mountain valleys of northern Idaho.

Just after the turn of the 20th century, northern Idaho began to attract more than the miner and logger. Recreation took on a new importance. A country club complete with golf course began operation at Hayden Lake in 1907. Trainloads of vacationers from Spokane would head for the lake each weekend, and some stayed all summer. Coeur d'Alene Lake was another popular destination.

The Great Depression of the 1930s brought hard times everywhere. The New Deal was particularly evident in Idaho. There were more Civilian Conservation Corps (CCC) camps in Idaho than any other state except California. Many of the camps were located on Forest Service lands, where the men built trails and lookouts, planted trees and worked on other conservation projects.

The advent of World War II drew Idaho out of the economic slump. One of the largest naval camps in the world was built in 1942 at Scenic Bay on Lake Pend Oreille. At one time 776 buildings were constructed, and the camp was the largest community (in terms of population) in Idaho. Nearly 300,000 sailors were trained here. Later the camp and the land were turned over to the state of Idaho and are now part of Farragut State Park.

Balsamroot graces the slopes above Harrison Bay along Lake Coeur d'Alene.

The 1950s and 1960s were periods of slow growth and more people moved out of Idaho than stayed. A short boom in the 1970s turned sour in the early 1980s. In particular, the timber and mining industries went through major restructuring. Mills closed all over northern Idaho for a variety of reasons, including lack of demand due to high interest rates, competition with Canadian and southern timber sources, and increasing mechanization. The industry was cutting more trees, but employing fewer people to do it.

Similarly, the Silver Valley experienced some major retrenchment. In 1981, Bunker Hill Mine, one of the major employers in the region, halted operations. More than 2,000 residents of the Silver Valley lost their jobs.

Concurrent with the decline in these industries, greater attention to environmental concerns was overtaking Idaho and the rest of the nation. No longer could industry dump toxic wastes into rivers. Clearcutting of forests came under increasing scrutiny. Concerns about endangered species, clean air, and forest roads all vied for the public's attention and sometimes incurred wrath.

With so much of Lake Country under U.S. Forest Service management, issues surrounding federal lands grew contentious. In 1972 Congress mandated that the U.S. Forest Service do an inventory of all its remaining roadless lands and make recommendations for potential wilderness designation. The Forest Service did two Roadless Area Review and Evaluations—RARE I and RARE II.

The Forest Service recommendations were supported by timber industry advocates, but almost universally condemned by environmental groups who held that the Forest Service left out many deserving areas during its review process. Before the Forest Service could move forward with roading RARE II areas not included in their wilderness recommendations, the state of California sued the federal government, claiming the Forest Service review process was inadequate and invalid. In 1982 a federal court of appeals upheld the challenge to the validity of RARE II in *California* vs. *Block*. The court ordered all timber sales in roadless areas to be put on hold until a site-by-site review was completed as part of Forest Management Plans or until the lands were specifically released by Congress. The order applied to northern Idaho forests as well.

To get around *California* vs. *Block,* the congressional delegations of western states including Oregon, California, Colorado, and New Mexico have introduced and passed bills designating some lands as wilderness, but releasing the rest for development. Although several Idaho wilderness bills have been introduced to Congress, partisan politics has thus far thwarted passage.

In northern Idaho the remaining large roadless lands identified on national forests include the Selkirk Crest, Salmo-Priest, Katka-Boulder, Scotchman Peak, Independence Creek, and Mallard Larkins. The controversy continues.

Even though federal land management issues remain unresolved, Lake Country's economy is on the rebound overall. Kellogg completed a major face-lift in the mid-1990s, revamping the entire downtown section of the community. With a $6-million federal grant, the city of Kellogg built the world's longest gondola, to the top of Silver Mountain ski area. It's possible to get off I-90, park, and jump on the gondola for the lift up the mountain. Few major ski areas are so accessible.

New hotels and resorts were built in Bonners Ferry, Wallace, Coeur d'Alene and Sandpoint. Coldwater Creek, a major mail-order house, recently expanded its Sandpoint operations. The key today is economic diversification, and Lake Country is making the transition to a healthier, more stable economy.

Concurrent with the new economic growth is a steady influx of retirees and migrants. For years people said, "You can't eat blue sky"—economies had to be based upon something like cutting down trees or mining ore. But increasingly, it is becoming apparent that people are willing to pay for blue sky, and pay a lot.

The lure of uncrowded streams, low crime and beautiful surroundings continues to tug at the hearts of Americans. With it comes controversy about growth management and land-use planning, as well as a new awareness of just how valuable things like clean water and blue sky can be. A new clean-up and management plan to maintain and improve water quality in Lake Coeur d'Alene is being drafted. Efforts to restore endangered species such as caribou and wolf continue. In some ways, despite the growing population, Lake Country just might be a better place to live in ten or twenty years than it was in the "good old days."

Climate

N orth Idaho's climate is heavily influenced by the Pacific Ocean. Only 300 miles from the ocean, the area has maritime air masses regularly sweep in bringing often cloudy skies and an abundance of moisture. Most higher elevations receive more than 40 inches of precipitation a year, which matches that of much of the Willamette Valley in Oregon or New England. Some of the higher mountain areas get 60 to 80 inches of moisture, mostly as snow. But besides being moister, maritime air masses are warmer as well. Nevertheless, northern Idaho has a relatively benign climate, particularly considering its far northern latitude.

Western redcedar in the Coeur d'Alene Mountains.

The major influence on northern Idaho's weather is the Aleutian Low. The Aleutian Low shifts southward from late September into June, moving the jet stream southward, bringing storms out of the Gulf of Alaska that sweep across the northern tier of states. These storms bring cool, moist air into the region.

With summer, the jet stream swings north, and northern Idaho is dominated by the Pacific High, which brings the dry, warm weather of summer. Thunderstorms are common—and often trigger forest fires.

You don't need to be a meteorologist to perceive that Lake Country has a wetter climate than most of the rest of the state. The lush forests and green meadows that linger all summer are ample evidence. But it always helps to put some numbers on these observations.

Sandpoint, at 2,100 feet in elevation, has a typical panhandle climate. Even during the hottest summer days, it seldom exceeds 90°, although temperatures of 100° have been recorded. At the other extreme, temperatures of -30° or below occur, but again they are rare, not the norm. Actually, the average minimum is usually in the low 20s. A total of 33 inches of precipitation falls a year—mostly in December and January, and primarily as snow. July is the driest month, receiving less than an inch of precipitation.

But just to give an indication of how different the climate can be in a short distance, Porthill is just slightly lower in elevation at 1,800 feet and is about 60 miles north of Sandpoint on the Canadian border, but it lies in the rainshadow of the Selkirk Mountains. While it gets only 21 inches of precipitation a year, overall temperatures are very similar.

There is also a gradual warming from north to south. Bonners Ferry is considerably cooler than Coeur d'Alene or St. Maries. The growing season in the south is as much as a month longer. In the south the frost-free season averages 150 days or more, while in the Bonners Ferry area the average is 120 days. Even with its relatively short growing season, however, the very warm, dry summers aid the ripening process, so that crops that might otherwise fail can still be grown in most summers.

Precipitation usually increases with altitude. That's because as an air mass rises, it cools and cannot hold as much moisture. The moisture drops as snow or rain. That's one reason mountains tend to have greater precipitation than areas with no relief. In addition, narrow mountain valleys receive more precipitation than wide, open ones. Air masses are in effect "squeezed" as they attempt to climb up and through the mountains, again dropping their moisture as they move up and over the highlands.

The Coeur d'Alene River Valley is particularly wet because it is oriented along an east-west axis—and hence receives a greater amount of moisture from the Pacific. Wallace, at the upper end of the Coeur d'Alene valley, gets 46 inches of precipitation a year—the most of any community in Idaho. This is the same as Eugene in Oregon's Willamette Valley. However, most of the higher elevations in the Coeur d'Alene Mountains, Selkirks and Cabinets receive considerably greater amounts than this.

Early morning fog on the Kootenai River by Bonners Ferry.

4
Coeur d'Alene and St. Joe

Coeur d'Alene is the hub of the subregion that takes in all of Kootenai County and laps over into nearby Benewah and Shoshone counties as well. With Coeur d'Alene as the center, spokes radiate out taking in the headwaters of the St. Joe River from the Montana-Idaho border, to the town of St. Maries and the Coeur d'Alene Indian Reservation, over to Post Falls, and on to the Rathdrum Prairie.

The name Coeur d'Alene, so the story goes, was given to the Shee Chu Umsh people by French fur traders who considered the tribal members shrewd bargainers with "hearts as sharp as an awl." The Coeur d'Alene people are an interior Salishan band, related to other tribes found in eastern Washington. Prior to the advent of the whites, the tribe followed a hunting and fishing tradition that was combined with bulb and fruit gathering.

There were approximately 700 Coeur d'Alenes around the time the first whites entered the region. As with all Indian people, the tribe's territory was gradually reduced as white people took up more and more of the land. In 1889, a congressional commission met with tribal leaders to settle a land dispute. As a result of the meetings, a 400,000-acre reservation was set aside, along with a cash payment to tribal members. However, the Dawes Act of 1887 had required each Indian to select 160 acres from the reservation and farm them. Lands not appropriated by Indians were frequently opened for white settlement, which is what happened to the Coeur d'Alenes. In 1909, more of the reservation was thrown open for settlement by whites. By the 1980s so much of the tribe's reservation lands had been sold off or otherwise lost that the Coeur d'Alene tribe controlled only 58,000 acres. The tribe has embarked on a program of land reacquisition and is currently buying up private holdings within the bounds of the reservation.

Even if the tribe's lands and influence have been reduced, its name is certainly well known. It graces a town, a national forest, a mountain range, a lake, and a river. Perhaps the best-known natural feature is Coeur d'Alene Lake, Idaho's second-largest lake. More than 30 miles long and averaging two miles wide, the lake seems like a long, wide river, which, in fact, is how it was created. The retreat of glaciers provided moraines that dammed the then north-flowing St. Joe River to create the water body.

Left: Lake Coeur d'Alene offers something for everyone.

Below: The stunning Coeur d'Alene Resort golf course, one of the many reasons people flock to Lake Country.

The lake was once a major cutthroat trout fishery. It is still a popular fishery, but now mostly for nonnative introduced species, including kokanee salmon, rainbow trout, northern pike, largemouth bass and Chinook salmon. The lake's fish population supports the largest nesting population of osprey in the western United States. Bald eagles also congregate on the lake, particularly in the fall to feed on spawning kokanee salmon. Eagle-watching near Wolf Lodge Bay is a major winter activity. As many as 40 birds at one time have been spotted in this area.

The south end of the lake is home to Idaho's first state park. In 1908, Senator Weldon Heyburn tried to set aside Chatcolet Lake near the mouth of the St. Joe River as a national park. When that effort failed, the land was given to the state and became the 7,800-acre Heyburn State Park.

As a centerpiece for the entire region's tourist and amenity-based economy, Chatcolet Lake attracts increasing concern over its water quality. Mining wastes from the Coeur d'Alene district were dumped into the South Fork of the Coeur d'Alene River for decades. The level of lead in the Coeur d'Alene River delta is among the highest ever recorded in the United States.

The Coeur d'Alene tribe has filed a lawsuit against mining companies for heavy-metal pollution of the lake. Nutrient enrichment of the lake is also a problem. Rural developments with septic tanks line the lakeshore, and phosphorus from fertilizers and detergents are leached into the lake from a variety of sources, including upstream farming on the lake's tributaries. In the mid-1990s, a draft water-quality management plan was released for public comment; the lake's water quality is getting the attention it deserves.

Coeur d'Alene, only 33 miles from Spokane, Washington, is North Idaho's largest town and commercial center. With more than 27,000 residents and growing, Coeur d'Alene is the seventh-largest city in the state.

Though it is rather far north, low-elevation Pacific Northwest maritime influences give this area a relatively mild climate, with a growing season of more than 150 days. Average precipitation is 24 to 25 inches a year, with a mean annual temperature of 48°. The mild climate and rich soils of the region support small farms, particularly in the Rathdrum Prairie area north of Coeur d'Alene and near St. Maries. These farms produce everything from wheat to grass seed.

The community of Coeur d'Alene got its start when Father Pierre-Jean DeSmet, a Jesuit missionary, met with a band of Coeur d'Alene Indians in 1842. Some believe the meeting occurred at or near the site of the present city. As a result of that meeting, a mission was built nearby, but later moved to Cataldo.

In 1859 Captain John Mullan (for whom the town of Mullan is named) began the survey and construction of a 624-mile military road from Walla Walla, Washington, across Idaho to Fort Benton, Montana, which was the upper limit for steamboat travel on the Missouri River. Frequent flooding, particularly near Cataldo, made the road impassable much of the time. Fourth of July Canyon along I-90 was named by Mullan's troops when they celebrated the holiday here in 1861. Floods in 1862 destroyed major sections of the road, and since there was no money allotted for maintenance, the road gradually disappeared. Wasteful military spending is not just a modern malady. Altogether Congress had spent $230,000 on the road, which was used only briefly.

In 1878, General William Tecumseh Sherman selected Coeur d'Alene as a site for a fort. A thousand acres on the shore of the lake were set aside and Fort Coeur d'Alene was constructed to guard the border of Canada and to discourage uprisings among the Indians. In 1887, the name was changed to Fort Sherman to honor the general. The fort was abandoned in 1900.

People began to settle around the fort, which offered employment and a ready market for produce. The discovery of gold, silver, and lead on the upper Coeur d'Alene River drainage induced a flood of miners into the area, some of whom settled by the shore of the lake, which was becoming an important trade link for northern Idaho. By 1887, there were more than a thousand people living around the garrison, and the city was incorporated that year.

A branch line of the Northern Pacific reached the city in 1887, and at the same time steamer boat service was initiated to the head of navigation at the Cataldo mission. The boats transported miners and supplies to the Coeur d'Alene mining district, while ore was moved downlake to the railhead.

Once railroads were established to the mining districts, steamboat travel focused on holiday excursions. Tours to the mission at Cataldo or around the lake were offered, with music, dining and dancing. As many as 2,500 people a day crowded the

Lake Coeur d'Alene at rest.

docks on weekends to ride one of the passenger paddle wheelers. The largest of these boats, the *Idaho*, was 147 feet long and could accommodate 1,000 passengers. Just after the turn of the 20th century, at the height of steamer travel, more than 50 boats plied the waters of Coeur d'Alene Lake.

By the 1910s and 1920s Coeur d'Alene was increasingly becoming a lumber town. Frederick Weyerhaeuser bought over 100,000 acres of Northern Pacific land grant holdings and began to cut the huge white pine that once cloaked the surrounding mountains. The Weyerhaeuser mill built just outside the city is now the site of a golf course, reflecting the changing economy of the community.

Coeur d'Alene was dubbed an "All American City" in 1991 by the National Civic League. Once a timber, farming and mining capital for the panhandle, Coeur d'Alene now has a more diverse economy. Coeur d'Alene's location on its namesake lake has generated new economic opportunities as an amenity-based town, attractive as a recreation/tourism center, as well as a home for people attracted to Lake Country for the quality of life.

The old Fort Sherman site is now part of North Idaho College, the only community college in the region. The campus has a relaxing, quiet quality that is also reflected in the nearby neighborhood.

The centerpiece of Coeur d'Alene is its waterfront series of parks. Tubbs Hill is the largest. The 150-acre natural area has a 1.4-mile trail along Tubbs Point. City Beach is the next park down the line, and it features a wide pathway known as "the promenade." The grassy, tree-shaded park is a popular place for picnics and swimming.

Rising between the two parks is the Coeur d'Alene Resort complex—the largest resort in the state north of Sun Valley. This

Above: Coeur d'Alene features a waterfront series of parks. City Beach is a favorite spot for a picnic and swim.

Left: Ah, to live here so close to City Beach.

development is symbolic of the economic transformation the region is undergoing as tourism becomes its lifeblood. While the names Sullivan and Weyerhaeuser were synonymous with early-day mining and timber development, the name Duane Hagadone is synonymous with today's development of the tourism industry in Lake Country. Among Hagadone's holdings is the impressive Coeur d'Alene Resort hotel and golf course.

The Coeur d'Alene Resort has become a fixture along the town's waterfront, in particular the golf course, which *Golf Digest* named "America's most beautiful" in 1992. One unique feature is the "floating" green, located in the lake. In addition to the golf course, the resort features the world's longest floating board-walk, which offers spectacular views of the lake. Some see the resort as a wave of the future—marking Coeur d'Alene as the "Tahoe of the North."

In August, Coeur d'Alene's famous Art on the Green weekend occurs beneath large ponderosa pine on the North Idaho College campus. The outdoor festival features arts, crafts, artists at work, and art shows.

Coeur d'Alene is the seat of Kootenai County, which is experiencing a population explosion. Congestion and rising real estate values are a few of the costs of this growth. For example, between 1970 and 1990, median housing prices in Kootenai County jumped from $13,800 to $64,800. And they have risen even higher since then. Part of this growth is spill-over from nearby Washington. Increasing numbers of people who work in Spokane live in Idaho and commute. On the other hand, this growth presents new economic opportunities and an alternative to declining resource extraction industries that once dominated the region.

Beyond Coeur d'Alene are a host of other communities with historical and recreational options. Post Falls, nestled along the Spokane River, immediately west of Coeur d'Alene, symbolizes the development overtaking the region. In 1970, 2,371 people lived in the community that grew to 7,349 people by 1990. But growth has only accelerated since then, and as of 1993, an estimated 9,500 were living in the town, with another 15,000 people within a five-mile radius.

Post Falls is named for Frederick Post, who purchased the site from the Coeur d'Alene Indians. Treaty Rock, located near the falls, commemorates the agreement between Post and the tribe.

Post built a dam and sawmill on the site. Eventually Washington Water Power Company purchased the dam to provide hydroelectric power to the Coeur d'Alene mines. The resulting power line was at the time (1903) the longest in the world. Besides its growing bedroom-community status, Post Falls is also home to Idaho's only greyhound racing park.

Just to the east of Coeur d'Alene is Cataldo, site of the Mission of the Sacred Heart, now part of Old Mission State Park. The Cataldo mission is the oldest standing building in Idaho and a registered national historical landmark. The mission was constructed in 1853 by the Coeur d'Alene Indians under supervision of Father Anthony Ravalli, to replace an earlier mission built at St. Maries. Constructed with hand-hewn logs secured with wooden pegs, the mud and grass walls are one foot thick. The mission was abandoned in 1924. Restoration efforts started almost immediately and in 1975 it became a state park.

Cataldo lies on the South Fork of the Coeur d'Alene River, which empties into the lake by Harrison. Highway 3 that runs between these two communities passes by 15 lakes that are popular with both anglers and birdwatchers. The highway makes a good backroads drive for those interested in a scenic alternative to the interstate.

South of Harrison is the St. Joe River. Cruising the "shadowy" St. Joe, possibly the world's highest navigable river, was once a popular past-time. Tugboats still ply its waters, pulling rafts of logs to Coeur d'Alene Lake where they are loaded for transport to mills for processing. The lower six miles of the river pass through the lake.

Levees poke up above the lake's surface. The levees were created by the 1906 construction of the Post Falls dam, which raised the water level of the lake slightly. It also flooded Hidden Lake, Chatcolet Lake, Benewah Lake and Round Lake, uniting them with Coeur d'Alene Lake. It is still possible to take a cruise up the St. Joe and pass beneath large old cottonwoods—which provide the shadows for the "shadowy" St. Joe. Along the way you'll see nesting colonies of great blue heron and one of the densest populations of osprey in the United States. However, there is increasing concern that speedboat travel and the resulting waves are causing severe shoreline erosion. That and sediments washed into the river from farmlands threaten to rapidly fill the south end of the lake. On the other

Right: The shadowy St. Joe, east of St. Maries.

Below: St. Joe Wild and Scenic River by Pack-saddle Campground, Panhandle National Forest.

side of the coin, the increasingly shallow lakes may produce an outstanding marsh wetlands complex that could be a boon to wildlife.

Indulging in the St. Joe River.

St. Maries, county seat for Benewah County, lies at the confluence of the St. Maries and St. Joe rivers. The town was originally established as a mission for the nearby Coeur d'Alene Indian Reservation. Once the railroad arrived, it became the hub of the local logging industry. Upstream from St. Maries is the St. Joe drainage; with campgrounds, historic sites, and great fishing, it offers wonderful backroads exploration. Some 60 miles of the upper river have been designated a Wild and Scenic River. It was once one of the premier fishing streams in northern Idaho. Early accounts regularly recount tales of locals catching 7- to 9-pound trout. Some parties hauled in 50 to 100 fish in just a few hours. The pristine upper portion of the river is managed as a Wild Trout Fishery.

The St. Joe drains the St. Joe Mountains, which separate

the Coeur d'Alene drainage from the St. Joe drainage. Most of the upper drainage is part of the Panhandle National Forest (formerly the St. Joe). Much of the crest of the range was burned in the 1910 fires. Some suggest that the rolling ridgeline of the range, which is made up of Belt Rocks, is reminiscent of the Smoky Mountains in Tennessee. Campgrounds line the river, and fishing access is easy from the road, which follows the river nearly to its headwaters. It's possible to drive over the Montana border and into St. Regis, Montana.

Floating the river is a good way to spend a few days. The lower 69 miles from Packsaddle Campground by Avery to St. Maries are either a Class I or Class II float, suitable for advanced beginner canoeists. Above Spruce Tree Campground are serious Class IV and Class V rapids which should be run only by experts.

The headwaters of the St. Joe include the 220,000-acre proposed Mallard Larkins Wilderness area, one of the premier wildlands areas in northern Idaho. Home to mountain goat, a number of glacial cirque lakes, giant mountain hemlock and shadowy groves of Western redcedar, the peaks of the Mallard Larkins region are just under 7,000 feet. Numerous hiking trails penetrate the region.

North of Coeur d'Alene are the communities of Hayden Lake, Rathdrum, Spirit Lake, and Athol. Much of this landscape is taken up with operating farms, and, increasingly, small subdivisions.

A special note must be made of the Rathdrum Prairie. Glacial alluvium covers the region, and beneath it lies the second-largest aquifer in the state. Recharge is by snow and percolation from lakes and streams. Twin, Spirit, and Hayden lakes all lack outlets, and the aquifer receives discharge from these and other water bodies in the region. Although a number of crops are grown here, the prairie is best known as a major Kentucky bluegrass seed-growing area. At the northwest corner of the Rathdrum Prairie lies Spirit Lake. The small town not only offers access to the lake, but is also home to the White Horse Saloon, the oldest continuously operating saloon in Idaho.

Across the prairie to the east and slightly south of Spirit Lake lies Hayden Lake. The lake is about 7 miles long; it has three campgrounds, and beaches open to the public. Along its shore is the F. Lewis Clark Mansion. Clark, who arrived in Spokane in 1884, amassed a fortune in milling, mining, and real estate. He built the 15,000-square-foot home in 1912 for a cost of over $385,000. The house and adjoining buildings were located on a 900-acre estate. In 1914, while wintering in Santa Barbara, Clark disappeared. Some thought he was murdered; others suggested suicide. His body was never found. By 1918, the Clark family fortunes were such that the mansion was given up to foreclosure.

Travel north along Highway 95 from Coeur d'Alene and Hayden Lake to the Silverwood Theme Park. The park has a reconstructed 1900s mining town, an amusement park, steam locomotives, and an airplane museum. A three-mile train ride is interrupted by a mock holdup.

A little farther on is Athol, once the site of a steam-powered sawmill. The town now serves as a way station for campers and others visiting Farragut State Park. To reach the 4,000-acre park, take Idaho Highway 54, the state's shortest highway.

To the east of Highway 95 lie the Coeur d'Alene Mountains. Most of the uplands are managed by the U.S. Forest Service as part of the Panhandle National Forest. An abundance of dirt roads offers weeks of backroads driving and camping opportunities. Few trails exist, but one exception is the Independence Creek Trail, a part of the National Recreation Trail system. At one time a wagon road followed the creek, linking Lake Pend Oreille with the upper North Fork of the Coeur d'Alene River Valley. The main trail and six side trails provide 34 miles of hiking terrain.

5
The
Silver
Valley

The Coeur d'Alene Mountains might hold the richest landscapes in the United States. Most people traveling on I-90 between Kingston and Lookout Pass don't realize they are passing through what was one of the most intensively mined valleys in the nation, and one of the early centers for organized labor. With the decline in mining activity, historical buildings are currently being renovated, and the area is increasingly being marketed as a tourist destination. The completion of the Silver Peak tram, and Silver Mountain ski area, promises to change the area's economy from one dependent upon resource extraction to a more benign use.

Wallace, one of the communities attempting to benefit from its turn-of-the-20th-century ambiance, is the seat of Shoshone County. The county takes in much of the Coeur d'Alene mining district as well as the upper St. Joe drainage to the south and the upper North Fork of the Coeur d'Alene drainage to the north. The "Shoshone" of the county name represents an error in geography. Legislators in the Washington territorial government bestowed the name upon the local Coeur d'Alene Indians, believing them to be associated with the Shoshone-Bannock tribe of southern Idaho.

Shoshone County was the first governmental unit in Idaho. Established by Washington Territory in 1858, it included all of Idaho north of the 46th parallel. Before 1882, few whites settled in the area now known as Shoshone County.

The forks of the Coeur d'Alene River both follow weaknesses in the earth's crust that have permitted the rivers to carve out their narrow canyons. These same faults also are responsible for the presence of mineralization. The South Fork of the Coeur d'Alene River, for example, follows the Osborn Fault, a 130-mile-long structural break in the earth's crust that extends into

Above: Wallace, established in 1884, provides early 20th-century ambiance in a magnificent setting.

Facing page, top: Coeur d'Alene River where it enters Coeuer d'Alene Lake.

Bottom: Courthouse in Murray. The discovery of gold in 1884 drew over 6,000 people to the region.

western Montana. Today's interstate follows this same crustal break.

All the Coeur d'Alene district mines are located in a large east-west–tending fault known as the Lewis and Clark shear zone. This series of faults marks the former continental plate boundary. Although faulting occurs throughout northern Idaho, the Coeur d'Alene area contains the greatest amount of deformation—hence mineralization.

The faulting also permitted mineral-rich solutions to intrude into the overlying Belt Rock formations that make up the Coeur d'Alene Mountains. These cooled and hardened to form the ore bodies of the Coeur d'Alene mining district.

The Coeur d'Alene mining district has produced more silver than anywhere else in the world. The district's 90 mines have produced over a billion ounces of silver, 8.5 million tons of lead, 3 million tons of zinc, and quantities of antimony, cadmium, copper and gold.

The Coeur d'Alene district contains the largest underground mine (the Bunker Hill), the deepest mine (the Star-Morning, over 7,900 feet deep) and the richest silver mine (the Sunshine) in the United States. Until the 1990s, 40 percent of the nation's silver came from the mines of the district. As of the mid-1990s, only two mines remained in operation, the Lucky Friday and the Sunshine.

The mines of the district are located in Precambrian metasedimentary Belt Supergroup Rocks—the same rocks that make up much of western Montana and the rest of northern Idaho. In the South Fork area the rocks of this belt are estimated to be 21,000 feet thick. Intruded into these ancient rocks are Cretaceous-age dikes and sills that contain minerals.

The first gold discovery along the Coeur d'Alene River is attributed to Andrew Prichard (for whom the town of Prichard is named). He found gold in 1878 on the South Fork of the Coeur d'Alene River at Evolution, near Osburn. A few years later, in 1881, Prichard's discovery of gold near Murray on the North Fork of the Coeur d'Alene sparked a rush to the area. More than 6,000 people were living in the mining region by 1884.

The gold rush to Murray died out by 1885, but miners attracted to the gold fields fanned out into the surrounding countryside prospecting for new ore bodies. In 1884, John Carten and Aleda Seymour staked a claim on a mineral outcrop along Canyon Creek at the site of the Tiger Mine near Burke, making it the first lode discovery in the mining district.

Soon other lode deposits were discovered, including the Yankee Lode destined to become the Sunshine Mine. New towns sprang up. Wallace was settled in 1884. Wardner had its first resident in 1885. By 1888 Mullan was established with more than forty homes and businesses. Kellogg followed in 1893.

Mines were one of the great mixing pots for workers. In the early 1890s the Bunker Hill mine employed 329 workers, including Americans, Irish, Germans, Italians, Swedes, Englishmen, Scots, Finns, Austrians, Norwegians, Frenchmen, Danes, Swiss, and a Spaniard, a Portuguese, and an Icelander. Such a mix of immigrants was typical of the frontier mining communities in the West.

Ore from the mines was originally smelted in San Francisco. It was taken by wagon to a steamboat landing near Cataldo, then by boat across Coeur d'Alene Lake. From there it was transported to a railhead in Rathdrum and taken to Portland, from where it was finally shipped by boat to California. The wagon road from Cataldo was eventually replaced by a narrow-gauge railroad that ran up the South Fork as far as Wallace, crossing the river 30 times en route.

The numerous mines all worked the same basic mineral-bearing rock structures that were broken up and displaced by the faulting that created the valley where the South Fork of the Coeur d'Alene runs. Since the ore-bearing veins went in multiple directions as a consequence of faulting and bending, it was possible for an adjacent mine to follow a vein onto the border of a claim of the neighboring mine. Litigation of mining claims became big business. For example, a locked door was once all that separated the underground shafts of the Bunker Hill and Last Chance mines.

Bunker Hill was the most famous mine in the valley. It was discovered in 1885 by carpenter Noah Kellogg, for whom Kellogg is named. Kellogg was grubstaked by a local businessman and doctor. After six weeks of prospecting, Kellogg staked out the Bunker Hill and Sullivan claims in Milo Gulch near the town that now bears his name.

In 1887, the Bunker Hill mine was purchased by Simeon Reed, a Portland, Oregon, businessman. One of the first things the new management did was to reduce the hourly wages of the miners. In reaction, the miners formed the Wardner Miner's Union and went on strike. In this, the first of many conflicts, the union managed to persuade management to reconsider. It was, however, just the beginning of labor troubles.

Bunker Hill was named for the Revolutionary War battle, but it became central to labor battles in the Silver Valley of the late 1800s and early 1900s. Today the remains of the mining operations are visible south of I-90 on the outskirts of Kellogg. The smoke stacks mark the company's smelter. More than any other, the Bunker Hill operation symbolizes the historical events that shaped the Silver Valley.

As early as 1884, there were disputes between labor and management over wages. In 1892, battles rose to a new height. Prompted by a collapse in silver prices and high freight charges, mine owners tried to persuade labor to accept a cut in wages. Labor refused and the mines shut down in January 1892. The lockout continued into spring.

Right: The Northern Pacific Depot, constructed partially of salvaged bricks, is Wallace's pride.

Below: A beautiful view from wherever you look—Coeur d'Alene Lake.

Finally, in May, the mines hired nonunion workers in Missoula, Montana, and by June had 800 nonunion employees at work. Mine owners had hired a Pinkerton detective to infiltrate the union. The spy had gained a position as union secretary. Union activists discovered the informant, and that, along with provocation from mine owners, led to the July 1892 dynamiting of the abandoned Frisco mill by union supporters. The mine owners called upon Governor Norman B. Willey, a mine supervisor himself, to declare martial law. Federal troops from Fort Sherman (Coeur d'Alene) and Fort Missoula marched into Silver Valley communities. For the next five months, martial law was in effect.

Union men suspected of participating in the uprising were confined to large outdoor prisons called bullpens. Nonunion workers were rehired and sent back to work. More than twenty union leaders were arrested for contempt of court and taken to trial in Boise. They were found guilty and given jail terms.

Outraged over what was happening to their fellow miners in Idaho, labor leaders in Butte organized the Western Federation of Miners to work for labor rights. The organization soon had many Idaho members. The labor vote became crucial, and some important labor concessions were made. We take many of these concessions for granted today, but the labor movement in Idaho and Montana set standards that were eventually adopted nationwide. For example, miners won an eight-hour day, the first labor group to do so. Companies were also not permitted to obstruct employees from joining labor unions.

Silver prices continued to decline. The Panic of 1893 set in motion a new spate of labor unrest. A number of railroads, including the Union Pacific and the Northern Pacific, went into receivership. By the end of 1893 more than 600 American banks and 15,000 businesses had failed.

President Grover Cleveland thought the source of the problem to be the Sherman Silver Purchase Act of 1890, which authorized the government to buy silver for coinage. Western silver-producing states were strongly supportive of the act because it provided them a ready market. Cleveland wanted to retain gold as the mineral of choice for coins, and he was able to get the Sherman Act repealed over the objections of Idaho miners and lawmakers. The mines used the recession to hire nonunion workers and reduce wages. The antagonism between labor and mine owners continued.

Rose Lake, southeast of Coeur d'Alene on the Coeur d'Alene River.

In 1899, labor troubles reached a still higher level of hostility. Nearly all the mines in the Coeur d'Alene district had organized into unions. The Bunker Hill and Sullivan Mining Company refused to recognize the union. In April, union workers marched on the Bunker Hill and Sullivan Mining Company offices in Wardner and demanded that only union men be employed and a minimum wage of $3.50 a day be set. The company suggested that workers who found the pay unacceptable could go elsewhere. The company posted armed guards and threatened to fire any worker who joined the union.

In response, on April 29 about a thousand miners from Mullan and Burke seized a Union Pacific train, loaded it with dynamite and proceeded to Wallace where more men boarded. The train then headed west to Kellogg. The miners routed a private

Left: Smelterville, once the site of Bunker Hill Mining operations.

Below: Remnants of mining days, Ninemile Canyon by Wallace.

army maintained by the Bunker Hill and Sullivan, and blew up a mine concentrator. A company worker was killed.

Idaho's governor declared martial law and troops were again called in to establish order. The state attempted to charge 400 men with murder and arson, and another 700 with conspiracy. The entire male populations of Gem, Burke and Mullan were arrested.

The state auditor issued an edict directing all mines not to hire union workers or risk closure. The Bunker Hill company doctor was appointed an agent of the state and authorized to issue work permits, thereby empowering him to decide who could obtain a job in any of the mines. No Western Federation of Miners union members were allowed to work in any mine unless they renounced membership in the organization. The Bunker Hill mine continued to require permits for twenty years. Hundreds of men were confined to the bullpen—some through the winter. Nine men eventually served time in prison.

In 1917, Bunker Hill built its own smelter, whose stacks are still visible in Smelterville, near Kellogg. In later years, sulfuric acid from the smelter was used with phosphate ore from southeastern Idaho to make fertilizer at Government Gulch. Gulf Resources, a chemical corporation, bought the complex of smelter, fertilizer plant and other metallurgical operations in 1968, and closed it in 1981. Two thousand workers lost their jobs. When the complex was closed it was producing 20 percent of the nation's refined lead and zinc, and 25 percent of its silver. The Bunker Hill mine contains over 150 miles of underground workings, the largest lead/zinc mine in the U.S.

Though Bunker Hill and the other mines provided employment to the Silver Valley for more than a hundred years, they also left behind a dangerous legacy. The smelter spewed forth toxic gases and ash. In 1976, in order to avoid costly alterations in operation necessary to reduce pollution, the company chose instead to construct taller smokestacks to disperse emissions over a larger area—thereby reducing the local concentration to levels more in keeping with federal air quality standards.

The solution by dilution reduced ground-level emissions; however, it didn't eliminate pollution problems for local people. The denuded slopes above Kellogg are stark reminders of the poisons that settled on the soils and pollutants that killed the trees.

In the 1970s it was discovered that smelter emissions were

affecting more than local flora. A study by the Centers for Disease Control in Atlanta found that 88 percent of 1,000 Silver Valley children tested had overly high levels of lead in their blood. Bunker Hill Company was sued for $20 million by several families claiming their children suffered brain and physical damage from lead emissions. Lead deposits at the school where the children played were found to be 160 times the level considered to be safe.

Today Bunker Hill is a Superfund site. Gulf USA, which owned the site, has declared bankruptcy, leaving taxpayers to pay for the cleanup of the area. A final settlement provides $20 million to the federal government for cleanup, but estimated costs are more than $100 million.

There are more environmental legacies as well. In the past, all of the mills in the district dumped mill tailings directly into the Coeur d'Alene River. Periodic flooding moved these metal tailings downstream and eventually into Coeur d'Alene Lake, contaminating the entire Silver Valley and a portion of the lake as well.

It must be recognized that the practice of using rivers as open sewers was not unusual at that time. Modern mining companies have adopted modifications and technologies to reduce environmental hazards. These, combined with much stricter environmental regulations, now guide mining development. The health hazards associated with earlier mining operations have largely been mitigated or eliminated. Although it is costly, environmental cleanup is proceeding, and the Silver Valley is already on the rebound.

The damaged environment was not the only mining tragedy in the valley. At about 11:40 A.M. on May 2, 1972, smoke was detected in one of the underground tunnels of the Sunshine Mine. There were 173 men in the mine at the time. Smoke quickly overcame some of the men and blocked the exit shafts. Rescuers were unable to get to the trapped men until May 8. The main shaft, however, was not reached until May 9, and by then the rest of the miners trapped in the tunnel were dead. Altogether 91 workers died, most of them from carbon-monoxide poisoning and smoke inhalation.

An iron sculpture of a miner, just off I-90, commemorates the miners who died in what was one of the worst disasters in hard-rock mining history.

Above: Prichard Creek in the Coeur d'Alene Mountains.

Right: Exposed Belt Rocks, near Wallace.

Another visual treat on Main Street in Wallace.

The Sunshine Mine had been discovered in 1884, and worked for 25 years by two brothers, Dennis and True Blake. Then the mine was leased for years before being sold to the Sunshine Mining Company. In 1931 a major silver vein was discovered as exploration went deeper than ever. The Sunshine Mine has produced over 350 million ounces of silver, the largest quantity from any single silver mine in the world. By comparison, the Comstock Lode in Nevada, one of the most famous silver mines, produced only 200 million ounces of silver.

The Lucky Friday Mine in Mullan is another example of a "late bloomer." In 1912, the mine was sold at a sheriff's sale for $2,000, and then again in 1936 for $120 dollars in back taxes. In 1938, Mullan garage mechanic John Sekulic purchased the mine for $15,000. He formed the Lucky Friday Mining Company, which began operations in 1942. As in the case of the Sunshine Mine, the ore got better as the shaft went deeper. Hecla Mining Company began to buy stock in the mine, and eventually merged with the Lucky Friday.

By 1989, the Lucky Friday Mine shaft was 6,100 feet below the surface. Instead of removing ore from above as is common in other deep-shaft mining operations, the Lucky Friday removes ore downward. As the miners sink on the vein they fill the resulting hole with concrete to prevent rock bursts. Rock bursts are dangerous explosions of rock that occur when the stone formed under intense pressure at depths in the earth is released by the mining operation. The mine shaft walls can literally explode.

Although mining continues in a few of the Silver Valley mines, the local economy is diversifying. One impetus to change was the 1989 development of Silver Mountain ski area in Kellogg. The mountain's 1,500 acres have 50 trails that receive up to 300 inches of snow each season.

One of the attractions is the gondola, which travels for 3.1 miles from the base village to the 3,400-foot rise to the Mountain Haus upper terminal. The ride offers spectacular views of the surrounding valley. Silver Mountain is much more than a winter resort. In summer, the gondola offers access to nature trails and mountain biking. One mountain bike route is 22 miles long, and all downhill. Summer concerts host big-name acts. The community of Kellogg itself underwent a $2.2 million facelift in the 1990s.

Silver Mountain isn't the only ski area in the region. Although Silver Mountain has its eye on becoming a large resort, Lookout Pass ski area, just 12 miles east of Wallace, is a comfortable family place that is seldom crowded. It has just one double chairlift and rope tow, but lines are usually very short.

Wallace is one of the most interesting Silver Valley communities. It was named for Colonel W.R. Wallace, who built a cabin on the site in 1884. It may be difficult to imagine now, but in 1890, Shoshone County had Idaho's largest population and Wallace was the state's third-largest town. The town's 1890 population included 28 saloon-keepers, ten lawyers, five doctors, but only one teacher. In 1910, the town was nearly cooked when the giant fires raced across northern Idaho. A third of the town burned.

The entire downtown of Wallace features some wonderful turn-of-the-20th-century architecture, whose centerpiece is the old Northern Pacific Depot. The bricks used in its construction were originally part of the Tacoma Hotel in Tacoma, Washington. Construction of the hotel was halted by the Silver Panic of 1898 and a fire finished it off. The bricks from the hotel were salvaged and some wound up in the Wallace depot.

Outside Wallace is the Sierra Silver Mine. It features public access to an underground mine and an explanation of mining technology. Just beyond is the Ninemile cemetery, near the center of which is a granite marker for three miners killed in the 1892 mining war at Gem.

Wallace is a central location for trips to a few other mining areas in the surrounding mountains. Just out of town is Burke, where the canyon floor is so narrow that store owners were forced to roll up their awnings or lose them to passing trains. The town is also the birthplace of movie star Lana Turner. The Hecla Mine, in Burke, was the original property of the Hecla Mine Company formed in 1891. A fire in 1923 destroyed much of Burke and Gem.

Above Wallace stands Mount Pulaski, named for an early U.S. Forest Service ranger. During the summer of 1910, extended drought, along with numerous lightning strikes, set off the largest fires in Idaho history. When it was over, more than 3.5 million acres had been scorched. Ed Pulaski was supervising a fire crew on Placer Creek south of Wallace during one of the "blow ups" of the 1910 fires. The fire roared up a hill and surprised the men. Pulaski led 42 of his crew into a retreat towards

Coeur d'Alene Lake offers a peaceful sunset.

A ride on the gondola at Silver Mountain in Kellogg provides 3.1 miles of spectacular view—and access to great winter skiing and summer hiking or biking.

Wallace, but their route became blocked by another fire. Pulaski, who was intimately familiar with the region, led his men to a nearby mine shaft just as the fire was about to overtake them. Panic-stricken by the smoke and flames, one of the men tried to bolt back outside the mine shaft. Pulaski drew his gun and ordered everyone to lie down. The fire grew hotter and louder, like a freight train bearing down the tracks upon the men. Even inside the mine shaft the heat was so intense that timbers caught on fire. With his hat, Pulaski dipped water from the mine floor and threw water on the burning timbers. Blankets soaked in water were placed over the tunnel entrance. Eventually they caught on fire too.

The smoke and heat finally caused Pulaski to lose consciousness. When he awoke hours later, there was fresh air circulating in the mine. The men were roused, and they set off for Wallace through the still smoldering and burning timber. By the time the men reached Wallace, their clothing was in parched rags; some had literally had their shoes burned off their feet. All of the men had burns, but they had survived. Today, a Forest Service fire-fighting implement with an ax on one side and a hoe on the other is known as a pulaski—named for the ranger who almost lost his life trying to stop that fire.

Not all of Lake Country burned to a crisp in 1910. The 183-acre Settlers Grove of Ancient Cedars near Murray is one such unburned site. These Western redcedars rival the California redwoods in size. Some of the trees are more than 30 feet in circumference and are hundreds of years old. The grove maintains a cool, moist environment that supports ferns, devil's club, and wild ginger. When the Forest Service first proposed setting aside the grove as a natural area, the Idaho Mining Association objected, claiming that no federal lands should be withdrawn from potential mineral entry for any reason.

You pass through Eagle on the way to the Settlers Grove. Though short-lived, Eagle once had two newspapers and a number of famous residents, including Wyatt Earp and his brothers James and Warren. Newly arrived from Tombstone, Arizona, the Earp brothers opened a saloon in Eagle in 1884. By December, a sheriff auctioned a tent belonging to the Earps for nonpayment of taxes. They, like almost everyone else in Eagle, had already left town for the next bonanza.

The Settlers Grove is off a newly designated Forest Service

scenic highway. The road running from Murray over Thompson Pass to Thompson Falls, Montana, will eventually be open year-round. Murray, once a major mining center, had a population of 5,000 people. Today it's nearly a ghost town, with only three businesses—two of which, in Old West tradition, are bars. The old Masonic Lodge, built in 1890, still stands, maintaining some of the architecture of the mining era.

Relics of the 19th century abound, including cabins. However, it is dredge tailings just outside of Murray that have rearranged the valley. The dredge was shipped from Alaska to Idaho in 1917. Electricity from Wallace powered the dredge, which for ten years chewed its way up the valley, sorting gold from the gravel in the streambed.

The North Fork of the Coeur d'Alene River continues on to Prichard, and eventually links back with the interstate by Pinehurst. The river is canoeable and fishable. It makes for a delightful drive.

Although much wealth has already been taken from the Silver Valley, the real wealth may yet to be found in the historic buildings and in beautiful mountain scenery. Ten or twenty years down the road, the major silver deposits being mined here just may be the coins in tourist pockets.

The northern part of the panhandle takes in Bonner and Boundary counties. Much of it is federally or state owned. For instance, 817,280 acres, or 73 percent, of Boundary County is managed by either state or federal land agencies such as the Forest Service. These federal and state lands are major assets of the counties, contributing greatly to the quality of life.

Lake Pend Oreille is the dominant physical feature, but other natural landmarks include Priest Lake, the Selkirk Mountains, Purcell Mountains and Cabinet Mountains. Sandpoint is the major population center in the region; other towns are Priest River and Bonners Ferry, plus a half dozen or so smaller towns like Moyie Springs, Clark Fork, Hope, Naples, and Porthill.

Nearly all towns and major roads follow fault-determined routes. Sandpoint lies at the junction of several major faults. The dominant structure is the Purcell Trench, separating the Selkirk and Purcell Mountains. Sandpoint, Naples, Bonners Ferry and Porthill all lie within this fault-induced valley. Clark Fork and Hope lie on the Hope Fault. Priest River and Coolin on Priest Lake lie along the Newport Fault.

The Selkirks lie immediately north and west of Sandpoint and the Pend Oreille River. The highest peak in the Selkirks is only 7,670 feet, but the range rises nearly 5,000 feet above the immediate lowlands. The range is part of the Kaniksu Batholith, a huge plug of granite formed deep in the earth and uplifted along faults that now define the range's eastern bounds. Heavily sculpted by glaciers, the higher parts of the Selkirks are dotted with cirque lakes, granite bowls, and pinnacles.

Lake Pend Oreille, Idaho's largest lake, is the major rec-

6 Lake Pend Oreille and Beyond

Above: Lake Pend Oreille at Johnson Point.

Facing page: A quiet moment at Lake Pend Oreille by Kootenai Bay east of Sandpoint.

reation attraction in this part of Idaho. Nearly 43 miles long and 6 miles wide, the lake has 111 miles of shoreline and is twice the size of Lake Coeur d'Alene. It is also one of the deepest lakes in the United States, with a recorded depth of 1,225 feet. The lake follows structural faults, but was also scoured and deepened by glaciers during the last Ice Age.

The lake was discovered in 1809 by David Thompson of the North West Company of Montreal. Thompson built a trading post, known as Kullyspell House, on the north shore near present-day Hope. The post was abandoned a few years later. At the time of Thompson's visit, the Kutenai Indians were living in the region. The tribe was originally a plains-dwelling people, driven into North Idaho by the stronger Blackfeet tribe. During the years when most tribes were being settled on reservations, the Kutenai people were left out. In 1974, they declared war on the United States to draw attention to their landless status. As a result they were granted an 18-acre reservation near Bonners Ferry, where approximately 75 tribal members now live.

Pend Oreille is renowned for fishing. The native fish were limited to bull trout, westslope cutthroat trout, and squawfish. In its pristine state, the lake was a fishing paradise where huge native fish were regularly taken. The United States Fishery Commission stocked the lake with nonnative fish—much to the detriment of the native species. Today, both bull trout and westslope cutthroat trout are heading for extinction due to habitat degradation as well as competition from introduced exotics.

Among the nonnative fish stocked in the lake are rainbow trout, whitefish, brook trout and lake trout (sometimes known as Mackinaw). The most sought-after fish are the lake's huge Gerrard race of rainbow trout (Kamloops). This subspecies was introduced from Kootenai Lake, British Columbia, in 1941. The fish is slow growing, but reaches immense proportions. The best time for catching the really big rainbows is in late fall once the lake's waters cool. The Idaho state record rainbow trout, a 37-pound, 5-ounce fish was hauled from Pend Oreille waters, as was a 32-pound bull trout. Fishing for kokanee salmon is also popular.

Much of the shoreline is part of the Panhandle National Forest, thus publicly owned. Most of the public lands are found along the steep southeastern shore and along the western shore from Bayville north to Camp Bay.

Sandpoint is the cultural and economic center of Bonner County. The town itself, which is located at the base of the Selkirk Mountains on a sand spit near the outlet of the lake, has a population of close to 5,300 people, and there is an even larger population outside the city limits.

In 1880, Robert Weeks opened a small trading post and store on the site. Twelve years later, the tracks of the Great Northern Railway reached the town. One of the railroad's employees, L.D. Farmin, platted the townsite in 1898. By 1906 three major railroads converged on Sandpoint.

The town owes its growth to the timber on the surrounding mountains and valley. With rail access to eastern markets, logging became big business. Great Lakes timber barons descended on northern Idaho, purchased huge tracts of land, and began sawmill operations. The first large mill was established in 1902 with Thomas Humbird as president. Humbird and his father, John, were partners of Frederick Weyerhaeuser. All men had well-established timber operations in the upper Midwest. Humbird and Weyerhaeuser built their first mill on the shore of the lake north of the present-day Edgewater Lodge. Humbird, Weyerhaeuser and other partners also obtained lands in the Priest River area and combined them with Sandpoint Lumber Company holdings, which started Sandpoint on the road to being a major lumber producer. Altogether the company had more than 200,000 acres of timber holdings.

In the early logging days, the present city beach site was a log yarding area. Logs were towed down the lake to the beach, where they were stored until needed. By 1925, Humbird Lumber Company averaged 1,300 employees. At one time, Sandpoint was known as the largest shipper of Western redcedar in the Northwest.

The Great Depression was a major setback for the region's fortunes. In 1931, the Humbird operations in Sandpoint closed, and a decade later the company's 120 acres of lakeshore property was sold to a California developer for $5,000. The rest of Humbird's land—over 200,000 acres—was put up for sale as home sites. Most of the private timber holdings were cut over by the 1930s. Since that time, much state and federal government land has been cut, with the timber industry today logging the steepest, most inaccessible lands.

In the early days of logging, most tree-fallers lived in iso-

Right: A swinging time at Cedar Bridge (Sandpoint) on Lake Pend Oreille.

Below: Priest Lake Golf Course.

A whale of a time at Sandpoint City Beach on Lake Pend Oreille.

lated logging camps in the woods. In 1934, the average faller earned $3.40 a day, of which $1.20 per day was deducted for room and board. Loggers worked six days a week. This was before chainsaws, so the work required two-man teams working with crosscut saws. The timber was so much bigger than today and the equipment so much less efficient that a crew often spent an entire day cutting and skidding a single tree. After the log was cut, it was branded with the company mark. Then horses dragged the logs; the Humbird Company, which had one of the best waterway systems, had extensive rail lines and flumes to move logs.

In a few areas, logs could be floated downstream in communal log drives to the mills. When the logs reached town, they were sorted by company brand and sent to the appropriate mill. The last log drive in Lake Country was on the Priest River in 1949.

Increasing mechanization reduced the number of men it took to turn out the same cut. The first changes came after World War II. Chainsaws were introduced into the woods. The first ones weighed 80 pounds; today's professional saws weigh between 15 and 20 pounds. At the same time, trucks came into widespread use, resulting in the spread of roads, such as the 10,000 miles of road on the Panhandle National Forest.

These roads have significantly affected wildlife. Studies in Montana and Idaho have demonstrated that elk will avoid heavily traveled roads, and grizzlies, in particular females with young, stay away from roaded basins—even years after the roads are closed. The same is true of other species, including wolf, lynx and wolverine. As a result of these findings, land management agencies such as the Forest Service have begun to close and gate logging roads once the timber harvest is completed. The road closures are being challenged by the timber industry and others.

Employment in the wood-products industry is declining—even though the amount of timber has increased—due to mechanization. Most of the big trees are gone—already cut. What's left is much smaller second-growth or high-elevation timber that would not have attracted a logger's attention a few decades ago. Today a faller/buncher can grip a tree, falling it in one motion. The tree is then delimbed and stacked, all by one person. Modern sawmills also use less labor. The result is that today's logging and sawmill operations use far fewer people. In 1957 nearly 38 percent of Bonner County's workforce was employed in timber. Today it is less than 15 percent.

Replacing timbering in terms of overall employment is the growing service-tourism industry. Sandpoint has always been a summertime recreation destination and it remains so today. Lake Pend Oreille provides swimming, fishing, sailing and boating opportunities, while the surrounding mountains offer hiking and miles of backroad driving. Sandpoint's marina and City Beach offer easy access to the lake and are favorites with locals on warm summer days. For rainy days or for those who would rather exercise by walking a mall instead of a beach, there is the Cedar Street Bridge. The window-studded mall spans Sand Creek, and includes everything from art galleries to restaurants.

Cultural activities abound as well. The Sandpoint Festival held for three weeks in midsummer features nationally known musicians. There is also the Sandpoint Arts and Crafts Festival, and Oktoberfest in autumn. The season winds down with the Winter Carnival held during the last week of January.

More and more, however, Sandpoint is becoming a year-round recreation town. In winter, the nearby Schweitzer Ski Area and resort provide snow sports opportunities. There are 2,350 acres of skiable area with 48 runs, and a vertical drop of 2,400 feet. The top elevation is 6,400 feet. Schweitzer is also the second-largest employer in the community, with more than 500 people working at the resort. Sandpoint is destined to mature and grow as a recreation center.

Although Lake Pend Oreille is the best-known water body in the region, it is not the only lake. When queried where they go for summer recreation, local residents picked Priest Lake, hands down. The glacier-carved, 19-mile-long lake has an intimacy that ocean-like Pend Oreille lacks. Cradled by the Selkirk Mountains, with heavy timber right down to the lakeshore, Priest Lake has the feel of a north woods lake—until you look up at the mountains beyond. At the north end of the lake is a two-mile-long thoroughfare that leads to three-mile-long Upper Priest Lake.

The state's record lake trout, a mammoth 57.5-pound fish, was pulled from Priest Lake. As in Lake Pend Oreille, the lake trout, introduced in the 1920s, displaced the native bull trout and westslope cutthroat that were once abundant in the lake. Kokanee salmon were introduced as a food for the lake trout,

Right: This lodge at Schweitzer Ski Area isn't just for those winter enthusiasts enjoying the 48 ski runs and 2,350 acres—Sandpoint has year-round recreation...

Below: ...but snow time is probably still the favorite.

RICK GRAETZ

Left: More of the Schweitzer Basin magic.

Below: Schweitzer provides a comfort level for everyone.

and for a while, the trout flourished. Then, in an attempt to improve the lake-trout fisheries, mysis shrimp, a freshwater crustacean, was introduced as food for kokanee salmon. Unfortunately, the shrimp ate the same food as young salmon. The salmon fishery collapsed, and along with it the lake-trout population. Priest Lake already essentially lost its native fish, and now it may lose its introduced fish as well.

Much of the shoreline is publicly owned. The east shore is largely managed for timber production as part of the Priest Lake State Forest, while the western shore is dominated by U.S. Forest Service lands. Numerous campgrounds along with a host of resorts cater to every desire from primitive camping to plush cabins.

Though summer is definitely the main season here, winter cross-country skiing, snowmobiling and dog sledding are becoming increasingly popular.

One of the most intense forest fires in recent history began just east of Priest Lake near Coolin. The 1967 Sundance Fire burned up over Sundance Mountain and down into the Pack River drainage and thence up the other side to Snow Peak. In only nine hours, the fire traveled sixteen miles and charred 50,000 acres. Such intense and rapid fire runs are unusual. Most fires creep along, occasionally flaring up and then dying back to a creep again. However, under special conditions of drought and high winds—exactly the conditions that fueled the Sundance blaze—a fire can take off and cannot be stopped. Observers stated that one minute no flame was seen; the next, the entire slope was on fire. This was the result of the turbulent winds, radiant preheating of the forest in front of the actual fire advance, and firebrands whirled aloft by the winds. Some spot fires were ten miles in advance of the main fire front.

Today you can see the aftermath of the fires. In the Pack River drainage, young trees now cloak the slopes. An abundance of snags is still visible. Snags are a long-term legacy of fires that provide homes to many bird species (approximately 25 percent of the birds in Lake Country rely on snags). Once the snags topple they are used for shelter by small mammals or they create habitat for fish if they fall into streams. Although fires are much maligned, they can more precisely be thought of as agents of change and transformation, rather than as agents of destruction. Indeed, from a biological point of view, fires are absolutely necessary for maintaining functioning forest ecosystems.

Just as fires are necessary for forest health, so are large old-growth stands. In fact, the two often go together, since the shade and high humidity found beneath the larger tree-stands often act as natural checks and firebreaks under normal fire conditions. One of these natural old-growth forest attractions lies just west of the lake. The Hanna Flats Cedar Grove provides a fine example of the kind of big trees that were once found throughout northern Idaho. The grove survived both a major forest fire and the logger's saw, since early loggers considered cedar virtually worthless compared to the white pine and other desirable lumber species. The grove is near the Priest Lake Ranger Station off Highway 57. The cool shadowy grove of big cedars is named for Jim Hanna who homesteaded the area in 1921.

Outboard motorboats, jet-skis, and loud fun seem to dominate Priest Lake during the day; early mornings and evenings, however, are enchanted periods when the Selkirk Mountains are reflected in the calm waters, while loons might be heard calling in the distance. For those inclined toward a more traditional watercraft experience, Priest River, a proposed Wild and Scenic River, is canoeable for 44 miles below the outlet of the lake by experienced boaters, especially during the low water of summer. The lush riverside vegetation and clear waters make this a gem of a trip.

Hiking the shore of Priest Lake on the 7.6-mile-long Lakeshore Trail, a National Recreation Trail, is popular, as is hiking the trail to Plowboy Campground on Upper Priest Lake, 2.5 miles up from Priest Lake. The very headwaters of the Priest River are part of the proposed Salmo-Priest Wilderness, an inland rainforest of giant cedar and hemlock. The Upper Priest River drainage experiences the highest precipitation of any area east of the Cascades. Some 20,000 acres in Idaho are proposed for wilderness designation, to be joined with 41,000 acres already designated as federal wilderness in Washington. Elevations range from 2,900 feet along the river to 7,548 feet on Snowy Top Mountain. A band of woodland caribou ranges through the Salmo-Priest and adjacent Selkirk Crest areas, along with grizzly bear.

The Priest River empties into the Pend Oreille River, which eventually joins the Columbia in Washington. Both the Priest River and the Pend Oreille River follow the Newport Fault. The rivers exploit the weak zone of crushed rock to carve out their channels.

The town of Priest River is becoming increasingly popular

Myrtle Creek Falls in the Kootenai National Wildlife Refuge.

as a retirement community. Retirees are attracted to the area because it offers outdoor recreation with a four-season climate in a community with little crime, affordable housing and access to Spokane.

Just west of the town of Priest River is Albeni Falls. A dam was constructed across the river here in 1950. The dam produces hydroelectric power and also regulates the water level on Lake Pend Oreille 25 miles upstream.

The highway from Sandpoint east to Montana is now a designated Forest Service scenic highway. It passes around the north end of the lake through the communities of Kootenai, Hope and Clark Fork. The highway follows the route of the Northern Pacific Railroad, now Burlington Northern, into Montana.

This route was not the shortest way to the Pacific, but it was the most lucrative for the railroad. In order to sweeten the

Above: Farms near Sandpoint safeguard the rural feel of the area.

Left: The Kootenai National Wildlife Refuge by Bonners Ferry is a fine place to appreciate the Selkirk Mountains.

pot for railroad construction, Congress gave rail companies alternate sections of public lands up to twenty miles on either side of the railroad route. This was later expanded to 30 miles. The Northern Pacific chose to build its tracks through northern Idaho to take advantage of the superior timberlands along the track route. By this means, railroad companies became huge timber holders throughout the West. Northern Pacific, for example, eventually gained title to 48 million acres of land—more than twice the size of the state of Maine.

Hope, 16 miles east of Sandpoint, sits on a hill overlooking the lake. The town is the site of a granite monument honoring David Thompson, the first white to visit the area. Thompson set up a trading post near here in 1809.

The community of Clark Fork was established in 1913 when lead-silver mines operated in the nearby mountains. Today the town is becoming a recreation-retirement community. Just beyond Clark Fork is 7,000-foot Scotchman Peak, part of the Cabinet Mountains. The peak rises nearly 5,000 feet above the community. The trail to the top is steep and without water, but the views from the summit are tremendous. You can see three states and Canada. The glaciated peak is part of an 89,000-acre proposed wilderness straddling the Montana-Idaho border that harbors mountain goat, elk, wolverine, and an occasional grizzly bear.

Highway 95 goes north from Sandpoint to Bonners Ferry and eventually the Canadian border. Along the way, you pass the turnoff for the Pack River. A road follows the stream back into the heart of the Selkirk Mountains, offering camping as well access to a number of high alpine lakes. The lower portion of the Pack River is canoeable.

Bonners Ferry is 38 miles north of Sandpoint and just 24 miles south of Canada. Located at 1,810 feet on the Kootenai River, the town takes its name from Edwin Bonner, who operated a ferry here during the 1864 gold rush to British Columbia's Kootenai country. The ferry cost 50¢ per person and $1.50 for a horse—a considerable amount of money in those days.

The Kootenai River headwaters are in the Canadian Rockies. The river flows south into Montana, then west to Bonners Ferry where it travels north back to Canada along the floor of the Purcell Trench. The river is so gentle that it's possible to travel from Bonners Ferry north to Canada's Kootenai Lake in a rowboat.

The river is home to the Kootenai River white sturgeon, which grows to immense size; it can attain a length of 10 feet and a weight of 1,000 pounds. This long-lived species was recently listed as endangered. The construction of Libby Dam on the Kootenai River in Montana has reduced the flood flows the fish requires for spawning. The U.S. Fish and Wildlife Service is requiring that spring flows be maintained for three years out of every ten in order to stimulate spawning by the species.

Straddling the river, Bonners Ferry has a quiet charm. It is the county seat for Boundary County. Like the rest of Lake Country, the Bonners Ferry area has experienced growth. In 1970 there were 5,484 people living here, and by 1990, 8,332 called the county home. The population density is now 6.6 people per square mile.

The climate is relatively moderate, with 24.5 inches of precipitation a year and 130 frost-free days. The mean January temperature is 25°, while the July mean is 67°. Winters, however, are long and cloudy.

As in the rest of Lake Country, logging the surrounding mountains is one of the important industries. Farming also constitutes a major land use. The rich soils along the Kootenai River support hops, wheat, barley, and other crops. There are also 17 nurseries growing everything from seedlings to large trees for retailing.

The largest employer in the county is government, followed by retail and wholesale trade. Tourism is growing, while the timber industry, once the main employer in the region, is declining.

In mid-July the town celebrates Kootenai River Days with a fiddlers' contest, dances and other events.

East from Bonners Ferry, Highway 2 heads toward Libby, Montana. The small town of Moyie Springs sits above the gaping gorge of the Moyie River. Just upstream lies Moyie Falls, whose dam produces hydroelectric power for Bonners Ferry. The Moyie River offers a challenging whitewater canoe run. The river is paralleled up to the Canadian border by a dirt Forest Service road. Several campgrounds are located along it, including Meadow Creek, former site of a logging town. Near the upper end of the river is Copper Falls, a long thin cascade set in a mossy canyon. A short trail leads to a viewing point.

Five miles outside Bonners Ferry is the Kootenai National Wildlife Refuge. The 2,774-acre refuge is an important stopover

Left: One of Sandpoint's many pleasant places to enjoy a sunny day.

Below: Between breezes at Sandpoint on Lake Pend Oreille.

Facing page: Lake Pend Oreille from Minerva Point.

for waterfowl migrating north and south with the seasons. A total of 230 bird species and 45 mammal species frequent the refuge. One of the reasons the refuge was purchased was to mitigate the losses created by the wetlands draining and dike construction that occurred as part of 1920s reclamation projects. A drive a couple of miles up the Myrtle Creek road to an overlook offers spectacular views of the Kootenai River Valley, the refuge and the town of Bonners Ferry.

The northern part of Idaho is a key piece in a larger goal of ecological restoration. The region, termed the Greater Cabinet-Yaak-Selkirk Ecosystem, extends into British Columbia, providing a link with the North Cascades and the Northern Rockies. Although significantly altered by human modifications, primarily logging roads, the area is still lightly populated, and most of the human habitation is confined to the valleys. Indeed, compared to the turn of the 20th century when logging and mining camps were scattered throughout the mountainous portions of the region, the uplands of today have fewer people. In addition, there are still roadless patches that, if connected by corridors where road closures and human activities are restricted to some extent, can still serve important biological objectives. Some of the key roadless areas are found in the Selkirk Crest, Buckhorn Ridge in the Purcells, Katka-Boulder Mountain and Scotchman Peak in the Cabinets. Linked together, they can provide a series of habitat islands connected by "bridges."

One of the largest of these proposed wildlands core areas lies above the Kootenai National Wildlife Refuge. The Selkirk Mountains of Idaho are just the southernmost extension of a 250-mile range that extends far up into Canada. The glaciated peaks and dense forests harbor the last relict herds of woodland caribou. The endangered caribou feed on lichens that grow in old-growth forest stands in the subalpine reaches of the range. With the heavy logging that has removed much of the mature timber and with the easy access created by logging roads that has increased poaching, the caribou is barely holding on. Approximately forty-nine caribou are thought to remain.

Nearly every major drainage in the Selkirks has been logged and roaded. One exception is Long Canyon. The glaciated 18-mile-long canyon is densely forested for its entire length, from its mouth on the Kootenai River Valley to nearly the crest. It is part of the proposed 41,000-acre Long Canyon-Selkirk

Crest wilderness. The middle third of the canyon is dominated by large-diameter old-growth forest. Long Canyon connects with the Selkirk Crest that runs north and south with twenty-four alpine lakes scattered among glaciated bowls and peaks.

Another roadless area centered on Katka Peak/Boulder Mountain lies just south of Bonners Ferry in the Cabinet Mountains. It is visible from the highway between Bonners Ferry and Moyie Springs. The 43,000-acre roadless area features steep canyons and several ridgeline trails, and includes 6,298-foot Boulder Mountain.

Most of the Purcell Mountains have been roaded and developed; however, a small 31,000-acre roadless area called Buckhorn Ridge straddles the Montana-Idaho border. The higher ridges still sport silver snags, relics of a fire that swept through the country decades ago. The open ridges make for easy hiking.

To those seeking charm and quiet, this part of the state offers rich rewards.

Another look, in the unlikely event you aren't convinced that Couer d'Alene's beauty is unique.

Index

Italic numerals indicate photographs

Evening beauty in Palouse country, near St. Maries.

Above: Selkirk Mountains rise over the Kootenai Refuge.

Top: The remote Moyie River near Meadow Creek in the Purcell Mountains.

George Wuerthner has worked as a biologist, teacher, university instructor, park ranger and guide. He is a full-time freelance writer and photographer. Among his 17 books are American & World Geographic's Idaho Mountain Ranges; Alaska Mountain Ranges; Forever Wild: The Adirondacks; Nevada Mountain Ranges; and California's Sierra Nevada. He writes a regular column on environmental issues in the Rockies for Wyoming's Casper Star Tribune. His photographs have appeared widely in everything from National Geographic to Arizona Highways. He contributes to dozens of calendars annually, and has had six signature calendars, including an Idaho Scenic Calendar published by Westcliffe Publishers.

Wuerthner and his wife, writer and wildlife biologist Mollie Matteson, and their daughter currently live in Eugene, Oregon.